A WALK OF FAITH

A WALK OF FAITH

SELWYN HUGHES

CWR

Originally published in 2006 as *Walking in Faith* by CWR, Waverley Abbey House,
Waverley Lane, Farnham, Surrey GU9 8EP, UK. Registered Charity No. 294387.
Registered limited company No. 1990308. Reprinted 2007.
Published in this format 2011 by CWR.

The excerpts in this compilation were taken from issues of *Every Day with Jesus*
by Selwyn Hughes, previously published as Jan/Feb, Mar/Apr, May/Jun, Jul/Aug,
Sep/Oct 1982 and Jan/Feb 1983.

See back of book for list of National Distributors.

Unless otherwise indicated, all Scripture references are from the Holy Bible:
New International Version (NIV), copyright © 1973, 1978, 1984 by the International Bible
Society.

Other Scripture quotations are marked:
RSV: Revised Standard Version, © 1965, Division of Christian Educastion of the National
Council of the Churches of Christ in the United States of America.
TLB: The Living Bible, © 1971, 1994, Tyndale House Publishers.
AV: The Authorised Version.
NKJV: New King James Version, © 1982, Thomas Nelson Inc.
Moffatt: The Moffatt Translation of the Bible, © 1987, Hodder & Stoughton.
Amp: The Amplified Bible Old Testament copyright © 1965, 1987 by the Zondervan
Corporation. The Amplified New Testament copyright © 1958 by the Lockman Foundation.
Used by permission.
Phillips: J.B. Phillips The New Testament in Modern English, © 1960, 1972,
J.B. Phillips, Fount Paperbacks.
Translator's: Translator's New Testament, © The British and Foreign Bible Society, 1996.
Williams: Williams Translation

Concept development, editing, design and production by CWR
Printed in Finland by Bookwell
ISBN: 978-1-85345-603-9

CONTENTS

'THE BLESSED HOPE'

FOR READING AND MEDITATION

Titus 2:1–15

'… we wait for the blessed hope – the glorious appearing of our great God and Saviour, Jesus Christ …' (v.13)

Is the return of Jesus Christ imminent? Will Christ's coming take place in our time? Are we truly living in the last days?

In an age that is growing darker and darker, the truth of Christ's return to this world is a ray of hope that shines like an ever-brightening beam. True peace will only come to this world when Christ returns to rule and reign as King of kings and Lord of lords. How thankful we Christians ought to be that in the midst of the world's dark and dismal problems, we have a hope for the future.

Father, the kingdoms of this world are being shaken. Thank You that I have been born into a kingdom which is unshakeable. Amen.

'GLORY TO MAN IN THE HIGHEST'

FOR READING AND MEDITATION

Romans 1:18–25

'They … worshipped and served created things rather than the Creator …' (v.25)

The past one hundred years has demonstrated, as no other period in history, the futility of trying to organise life without God. Men have tried on a massive scale to thrust God out of the universe and institute a religion of humanity. Because modern men and women found it hard to believe in God, they transferred their faith to man. 'Glory to man in the highest' is their creed, coupled with, 'Let us eat, drink and be merry for tomorrow we die'. Our times are spiritually and morally bankrupt and have exhausted the spiritual capital left over from previous centuries. There is no hope for the world spiritually unless we see a worldwide revival, or Christ comes again.

O God, I long for Your kingdom to be fully established on this earth. Amen.

JANUARY 3

THE WORLD IN PERIL

FOR READING AND MEDITATION

Romans 3:10–18

'... ruin and misery mark their ways ...' (v.16)

People liked being told that there was no such thing as original sin, that the Golden Age was inevitable and that, by gradual steps, mankind would move unaided to perfection. This belief made redemption unnecessary, emptied the cross of meaning and made the Church a joke. Then came two world wars, and still there is war in many lands. Is it not obvious to everyone that unredeemed man, neglectful of his Creator, through war and pollution is in danger of turning this beautiful planet into an ash heap? In an age of global pollution and nuclear weapons, the only hope for the world physically is the personal return of our Lord Jesus Christ.

O God, You, and You alone, can save this planet from ruin. Come soon, Lord Jesus, and save us from ourselves. Amen.

THE SECOND COMING

'A POLITICIAN'S NIGHTMARE'

Mark 7:14–23

'For from within ... come evil thoughts, sexual immorality, theft ... greed ... deceit ... envy ...'
(vv.21–22)

Today's world is a politician's nightmare. As soon as one problem is solved, a greater one arises. There are still some politicians who believe sincerely that one day the world will overcome its difficulties and we shall settle down into an age of peace and prosperity. This, in my view, is unrealistic. The Bible tells us that the human heart is filled with greed, lust, envy, jealousy, pride and selfishness, and these flaws in human nature will never be put right on a universal scale until Christ returns to rid the world of evil and establish His reign of righteousness on the earth. Unless Christ returns soon, there can be no hope for the world politically. His promised return is both deeply reassuring and doubly welcome.

Blessed Lord Jesus, help me to peer through the darkness of international strife and tension to catch the gleam of Your triumphant return. Amen.

DWINDLING RESOURCES

Genesis 1:26–31; Isaiah 24:1–16

'The earth lies polluted under its inhabitants ...'
(Isa. 24:5, RSV)

Conservationists tell us that our natural resources are dwindling and demand will soon exceed supply. Stephen Travis, in his book *The Jesus Hope*, says that the United States produces only 60 per cent of the oxygen it consumes and if we go on polluting we could reach the stage where there is no longer enough oxygen to support human life. We have littered the earth with indestructible plastics, poisonous chemicals and many other things; little realising that, by so doing, we are threatening human survival. Unless Jesus Christ returns soon, the inhabitants of this tiny planet may well annihilate themselves by their folly. Apart from Christ's return, there is no hope for the world ecologically.

Father, open the eyes of the world's inhabitants so that they may see that apart from You, there is no real hope for mankind. Amen.

HOPE – OR BLIND OPTIMISM?

Jeremiah 17:1–8

'Blessed is the man who trusts in the LORD ...'
(v.7, RSV)

The human personality cannot remain stable without a sense of true optimism or hope. Today, both young and old alike combine to reflect a pessimism concerning the future. Most people, when faced with such gloom and uncertainty, reach out for a substitute. They try such things as occultism, transcendental meditation, alcohol, sex, drugs, pursuit of wealth or fame etc. But they are false hopes. They pick you up but they soon let you down. Everything outside of Jesus Christ is blind optimism. He, and only He, can supply the human personality with the power it needs to function effectively in an age that is falling apart at the seams.

O God, I see that outside of You, my hopes are hopeless. Only in You is true security. Amen.

'RELIGION WITH A HAPPY ENDING'

FOR READING AND MEDITATION
Ephesians 1:1–10

'... gather together in one all things in Christ ...'
(v.10, NKJV)

We are seeing that hope is a necessity of life. Without it men and women cannot live effectively.

A Jewish rabbi said that the Jews are more a people of hope than a people of faith. He explained that although at times their faith was exceedingly weak, they never lost hope that one day they would become a recognised nation in their own land. 'Judaism,' said a rabbi, 'can justly be described as a religion with a happy ending.' Christians look out into the future without any doubt that God is going to have the last word in human history. Someone said of the apostle Paul that 'he was sure of God's happy endings'. With our eyes focused on the future, may the same be said of you and me.

O God, my Father, thank You for the sustaining hope of Your coming again to this world. Amen.

THE TWO ADVENTS

Daniel 7:13–14; Isaiah 53:1–9

'... that all peoples, nations, and languages should serve him ...' (Dan. 7:14, RSV)

For every mention in the Bible of Christ's first advent, there are eight allusions to His second advent. Many of the teachers in ancient Israel failed to differentiate between the two. The two passages before us today show quite clearly the difference between them. First, Christ would come as a suffering servant and then as a triumphant king. Why, we ask ourselves, did so many miss this truth? Perhaps it was because they leaned too much on their own understanding and allowed their passion for physical deliverance to blind them to their need for an even greater deliverance – the deliverance from sin.

O God, help me not to lean on my own understanding or thoughts about Christ's second coming. In Jesus' name. Amen.

'A FLAME IN MY HAND'

FOR READING AND MEDITATION
Jeremiah 23:23–32

'Is not my word like fire, says the LORD ...'
(v.29, RSV)

Christians believe in the second coming of Jesus Christ because the truth is clearly affirmed in the Scriptures. Some might object to this and say, 'But how do we know the Bible is true?' There are many 'proofs' that the Bible is true. However, Dr Martyn Lloyd Jones said, 'Ultimately this question of the authority of the Scriptures is a matter of faith and not of argument.' Before Dr Billy Graham went into the ministry, he wrestled with deep doubts about the reliability of the Bible. He says, 'But one day I decided to accept the Scriptures by faith. When I did this ... it immediately became a flame in my hand.'

Gracious Father, help me to accept the Bible by faith so that its power shall flow in me and through me. Amen.

THE SECOND COMING

THE 'PRINCIPLE OF PROBABILITY'

FOR READING AND MEDITATION

Isaiah 42:1–12

'Everything I prophesied came true ... I will tell you the future before it happens.' (v.9, TLB)

I s the Bible true and reliable?' One of the strongest objective arguments for the validity of Scripture comes from fulfilled Bible prophecy. Peter Stoner has utilised what is called the 'principle of probability' to passages such as Ezekiel 26:3–16 predicting the destruction of Tyre. All seven predictions came to pass despite a probability of one in 400 million. Biblical prophecy declares the events of the future with an accuracy that is beyond the capability of human wisdom or anticipation. Despite astronomical odds, hundreds of biblical prophecies have come true, and this, apart from anything else, is an impressive tribute to the authority and reliability of the Scriptures.

O God, help me to experience an unfailing confidence in the authority and reliability of Your precious Word. For Jesus' sake. Amen.

PREDICTIVE PROPHECY

FOR READING AND MEDITATION
Isaiah 46:8–13

'... I am God, and there is none like me, declaring the end from the beginning ...' (vv.9–10, RSV)

No man can accurately forecast the future. George Orwell, in his book *1984*, seems to be near the mark, but his predictions were merely those of a few decades in advance, not generations. Around 2,500 years ago, the Bible foretold events which are taking place in our day. For example, the formation of modern Israel. How was it able to do so? Examine the text at the top of this page once again and you will see. The eternal God, who stands above the march of time, sees and knows the end from the beginning and, in His wisdom, He has chosen to share with us certain things about the future that He wants us to know.

O Father, guide me when I come to puzzling and perplexing truths in Your Word. This I ask in Jesus' name. Amen.

HE TOLD US HIMSELF

FOR READING AND MEDITATION
Luke 19:11–27

'… he went on to tell them a parable, because … the people thought that the kingdom of God was going to appear at once.' (v.11)

The New Testament writers predicted Christ's coming, but also Christ Himself taught us that one day He would return. 'I will come again', He said (John 14:3, RSV). In the parable before us today, did you notice the phrase: 'A certain nobleman went into a far country to receive for himself a kingdom, and to return' (v.12, NKJV)? Amongst our Saviour's last words, in the book of Revelation, are these: 'Behold, I am coming soon' (22:7). Truly, as James Culross expresses it, 'If Christ were not to come, He would break His word.' Mary Warburton Booth sums up the feelings of all true believers when she cries: 'He tells me He is coming and that's quite enough for me.'

Lord Jesus, I never cease to thank You for the promise I know You will never break. Amen.

IT IS LITERALLY TRUE

Philippians 1:12–26

'... I desire to depart and be with Christ ...' (v.23)

Some Christians claim there is not a literal return of Christ. They suggest that Christ's coming really takes place when a Christian dies. According to Paul, when a Christian dies, it is not so much that Christ comes for him but that he (the Christian) goes to be with Christ. Others say that Christ's coming took place on the Day of Pentecost. 'He came back,' they claim, 'in the power of the Holy Spirit.' Didn't the angels say, when Christ was taken up into heaven from the Mount of Olives, 'This same Jesus ... will come back in the same way you have seen him go?' How did He go? Visibly and physically. And that is how He will return.

O God, save me from the errors and misconceptions that men attempt to spin around this most matchless truth. In Jesus' name. Amen.

THE SECOND COMING

'I'LL COME BACK FOR YOU'

1 Thessalonians 4:7–18

'For the Lord himself will come down from heaven … we … will be caught up … to meet the Lord in the air.' (vv.16–17)

I once read a feature entitled, 'I'll come back for you'. It was a touching story about a little eight-year-old girl whose mother was forced to commit her to the care of an orphanage. When they parted, the mother promised, 'It's only for a short while, my darling. Then I'll come back for you.' But she never did, and the girl was adopted by foster parents. The girl felt deserted and forgotten. The mother had had a tragic accident and was unable to return until years later, when she did come back and keep her promise. We may feel deserted, but one day Jesus will come back and fulfill His promise.

Father, nothing will ever prevent You from keeping Your eternal promise. I know You are coming back – for me. Amen.

'THE SIGNS OF THE TIMES'

Luke 21:5–19

'There will be great earthquakes ... fearful events and great signs from heaven.' (v.11)

Some of the signs that Christ and other biblical personalities give as pointing to the nearness of the second advent, are characteristic of every age – wars, earthquakes, famines and so on. However, whilst the Bible gives a list of general signs so that people in every generation might be 'kept on their toes', so to speak, there are, at the same time, special signs which, by their very nature, can only be clearly understood and interpreted as the end actually draws near. We must be careful not to take the biblical signs out of context and push them too far. We must be equally diligent also that we do not miss what God is saying to us.

Father, keep me from immature conclusions, and enable me to see the truth as You intended it. In Jesus' name I pray. Amen.

THE SECOND COMING

THE GLOBAL GOSPEL

Matthew 24:1–14

'… this gospel … will be preached in the whole world as a testimony to all nations …' (v.14)

The first sign of Christ's return is the 'Global Gospel'. Never, until our own time, has the gospel been truly global. There are two main reasons for this. First, never until our own age has the world been fully explored. Second, never until now have we had the means to communicate the gospel message across national and international boundaries through radio, television and other forms of mass media. Since the end of the Second World War, there has been an enormous acceleration in evangelistic endeavour, and we are seeing, without any doubt (to my mind at least), the truth of God's Word being fulfilled in our own day.

O Gracious God and Father, all things are moving to the climax of Your purposes. I am so thankful. Amen.

MULTIPLIED LAWLESSNESS

2 Timothy 3:1-5, 13

*'... the final age of this world is to be a time
of troubles.' (v.1, NEB)*

It is true that a certain amount of lawlessness has always
been present in the world, but the current epidemic of
crime and violence is greater than past generations. Billy
Graham says, 'Compared to when I was a boy, we live
life in reverse. The people are locked up in their homes at
night and the criminals are outside on the loose!' Some
historians are saying that this present society is the most
violent society in the history of the world. Can we not see
that even though lawlessness has been a characteristic of
every age, it has never been seen on such a worldwide scale
as at present.

**Father, thank You that despite the gloom of the age I
can still reach out to touch others by my friendliness
and love. Amen.**

'AS IT WAS ... SO IT WILL BE'

Matthew 24:36–44

- -

'As it was in the days of Noah, so it will be at the coming of the Son of Man.' (v.37)

Jesus said, 'As it was in the days of Noah, so it will be at the coming of the Son of Man.' When the conditions before the Flood are repeated in history, the end is near, says Jesus. What happened in Noah's day? There was an abnormal emphasis on sex, food and physical pleasure. Today we are facing the same problem. The world is on an immoral binge, such as was not known even in the days of ancient Rome. Here in the West, people have become gluttons. Why, even our dogs are better fed than millions of people in the Third World!

Father, bless the preaching of Your Word so that people might be saved and find hope in You. For Jesus' sake. Amen.

'THE WAY OF CAIN'

FOR READING AND MEDITATION

Jude 3–16

'They have taken the way of Cain ...' (v.11)

Another feature of Noah's day was a falling away from the faith. The Bible talks about those who have taken the way of Cain. Cain initiated the violence and lawlessness that caused God to send the Flood. Cain believed in God. He had heard the Almighty speak to him from heaven. His error was that He decided to ignore God's requirement for a blood sacrifice and instead attempted to substitute a humanistic type of religion. Isn't this what is taking place all around us today? Multitudes who believe in God are, nevertheless, going the way of Cain. They ignore God's plan of salvation – the cross – and substitute for it a religion of good works.

Father, thank You that I am saved and that I can face the future with confidence and hope. Amen.

'CAN THESE BONES LIVE?'

FOR READING AND MEDITATION
Ezekiel 37:15–22

'I will gather them from all around and bring them back into their own land.' (v.21)

Another sign of Christ's coming is the establishing of the State of Israel and the return of the Jews to their promised homeland. In May 1948 the modem State of Israel was established and in June 1967 Jerusalem became a Jewish city for the first time since 586 BC. The Bible, of course, predicted that one day this seemingly dead nation would spring to life. God asks the prophet, 'Can these bones live?' In other words, how can a nation dispersed, ridiculed and driven to the ends of the earth be brought back together again? This is one of the greatest evidences in modern times of God's ability to fulfil His prophetic word.

O Father, day by day, my faith in the outworking of Your Word is being deepened and strengthened. Amen.

'THE TIMES OF THE GENTILES'

Luke 21:20–28

'... Jerusalem will be trodden down by the Gentiles, until the times of the Gentiles are fulfilled.'
(v.24, RSV)

Jesus talks about 'the times of the Gentiles' being fulfilled. What does He mean? Some Bible scholars think that the times of the Gentiles began in 86 BC when Nebuchadnezzar sacked the city, pulled down the sanctuary and deported some of the Jews to Babylon (2 Kings 25:8–11). From that time to this present generation, Jerusalem has been under the domination of Gentile forces. However, on the morning of 7 June 1967, Israeli troops retook Jerusalem. When this happens, Jesus says ... then they shall see the Son of Man. I ask myself, along with thousands of other Christians as we witness the miracle of Israel: How close must Christ's coming be?

Father, my whole being longs to find out more of Your truth and walk in it. In Jesus' name I pray. Amen.

THE SECOND COMING

IS CHRIST WITH US NOW?

Matthew 18:15–20

'For where two or three are gathered in my name, there am I in the midst of them.' (v.20, RSV)

Some ask: 'If Christ went back to heaven following His resurrection and is to return at the end of the age, does this mean that, at the present time, He is now absent from the world and from His Church?' Far from it! He said 'I am there with them' (v.20, GNB) – invisible but really there. It is the risen Christ Himself in our midst when we meet in His name. He is the centre of that fellowship, alike in the congregational as in the cosmic sense. The Church here on earth finds its cohesion in the magnetism of an unseen yet ever-present Lord.

Father, I am so thankful that I can still enjoy Christ's presence with me here on earth. Thank You, Father. Amen.

A PUZZLING PARADOX

John 14:16–26

'But the Counsellor, the Holy Spirit ...
will teach you all things ...' (v.26)

How are we to understand the puzzling paradox set out in the Scriptures which tells us that one day Christ will return to this world, yet also affirms that He is here with us – right now? The answer is not easy to grasp but hinges on what happened at Pentecost. Jesus refers to the Holy Spirit as 'He' and so, by using the personal pronoun, indicates that the Spirit is not an influence but a Person with the qualities of will, intelligence, emotion and so on. Make no mistake about it, when we come into contact with the Holy Spirit, we come into contact with a Person who is co-equal with God in rank, status and power.

Holy Spirit, I see You are a Person with whom I can commune and from whom I can draw endless power. Amen.

THE SECOND COMING

ANOTHER PUZZLING PARADOX

John 7:32–39

'Up to that time the Spirit had not been given, since Jesus had not yet been glorified.' (v.39)

Many times in the Old Testament, we see evidence of the Holy Spirit at work. What then does Scripture mean when it says that the Spirit will not be given until after Jesus' glorification? The answer is, of course, that although the Spirit was at work in the world prior to the coming of Christ, He was not fully active because there was no perfect vehicle through whom He could reveal Himself. When once He achieved a particular purpose, the Holy Spirit returned to heaven, waiting, as did the dove in Noah's time, for a point and a place on which He could not only rest, but remain.

O Father, I am so thankful that I am living in the age of the Spirit, where He is with me always. Thank You, Father. Amen.

'A NEW AND LIVING WAY'

FOR READING AND MEDITATION
Hebrews 10:16–27

'... we have confidence to enter the Most Holy Place by the blood of Jesus, by a new and living way ...'
(vv.19–20)

ecause Jesus came from God and returned to God, He has opened up a highway between heaven and earth which is paved with the footprints of redeeming love. Once this massive engineering feat was accomplished by Christ through His efforts on Calvary and by the resurrection, the way was then open for the Holy Spirit to follow. Can you see now why the Spirit could not be given until Jesus was glorified? 'Pentecost,' says Stephen Olford, 'could not be a reality until Calvary was a finality.' It is along a highway sprinkled with the precious blood of our Lord Jesus Christ that the Holy Spirit came to give Himself fully to the world.

Father, thank You for opening up this communication link between heaven and my heart. Eternal praise be to Your name for ever. Amen.

A PROGRESSIVE UNFOLDING

Joel 2:28–32

'… I will pour out my Spirit on all people.' (v.28)

Those who go astray in relation to the teaching of the Holy Spirit more often than not base their conclusions on Old Testament revelation. For example, the Spirit of God inspired Samson who killed many Philistines (Judg. 14:19). The Old Testament must not be considered to be the full and final declaration of God's purposes and revelation. The teaching of the Spirit in the Old Testament was progressive – it was a point in a line leading forward to the full and final revelation expressed through Jesus. If a person claims to be possessed by the Holy Spirit but doesn't act like Jesus, then it isn't the Holy Spirit who possesses him but some other spirit.

Lord Jesus, I see that the Spirit is the 'Holy' Spirit, and in harmony with the nature of holiness that I see in You. Amen.

ULTIMATE CHARACTER

FOR READING AND MEDITATION
Acts 2:29–40

'... he has received ... the promised Holy Spirit and has poured out what you now see and hear.' (v.33)

It is only in Jesus that we see ultimate character revealed. The disciples who had walked with Jesus seemed to have the idea that Messianic power would be manifested in an overwhelming display that would compel obedience. But the reality was different! He overcame His enemies by loving them. When the Spirit came to them at Pentecost, they knew then that this was ultimate power with ultimate character. The Spirit could not have been given in the days of Christ's humiliation; that would have set the wrong pattern. He could be given only in the day of His glorification; that set the right pattern.

Father, I thank You that You conquered everything and, through Your Spirit, so can I. Blessed be Your name for ever. Amen.

THE SECOND COMING

CHRIST – UNIVERSALISED

John 16:5–15

'... the Spirit will take from what is mine and make it known to you.' (v.15)

If Christ is going to return, in what sense can it be said that He is with us now? The Holy Spirit, in a sense, has universalised Jesus; that is to say, He makes His life and presence known to millions of His followers across the face of the earth at one and the same time. Because we are physical beings, we long to see the face of our master, but that joy must still await us. In the meantime, the Holy Spirit brings the life, the reality and the joy of Christ's presence into our hearts so that although we know He is not physically present, we experience His spiritual presence in a manner that is beyond expression.

Father, I am so thankful that through the Holy Spirit's ministry, Jesus is with me every hour of every day. Amen.

SHALL A MAN LIVE AGAIN?

FOR READING AND MEDITATION
Job 14:1–14

'If a man dies, will he live again?' (v.14)

What happens to those who 'die in the Lord' prior to His coming? Do they consciously enjoy the presence of Christ or are they in a state of utter oblivion, awaiting the final resurrection? Various answers are given to the question of death. One view of death says that we are no more important than a combination of chemicals and death is complete annihilation. This amounts to a total denial of all expectation of personal continuance in a world to come. By this view, life is cheapened while it lives and it is extinguished when it dies. Anything that cheapens life in this way is a cheap view of life.

Father, thank You I am not just a chemical combination but I am made by You and for You. Amen.

THE SECOND COMING

REINCARNATION – A MYTH

FOR READING AND MEDITATION

Matthew 11:1–15

'... *if you are willing to accept it, he is Elijah* ...'
(v.14, RSV)

Some believe in reincarnation. They say that since this life is too short and too indeterminate to work out our final destiny, we will come back again – be reborn on a higher or lower scale of existence, according to our deeds. The Bible does not support this view. Jesus simply said that John came in the spirit and power of Elijah. He was not saying that John was Elijah. The fact that Moses and Elijah appeared on the Mount of Transfiguration proves survival, but not by any stretch of the imagination can it prove reincarnation. The human race does not need reincarnation but regeneration in His Incarnation.

O Father, open up Your Word to me so that I shall know the truth. In Jesus' name. Amen.

IS THERE A SECOND CHANCE?

FOR READING AND MEDITATION
Genesis 18:23–33

'Will not the Judge of all the earth do right?' (v.25)

niversalism teaches that everybody will be finally saved, but God will not save a person against their will. I do not believe in a 'second chance', but I do believe in an adequate chance. Infants, the mentally incapable, those dying before reaching the age of responsibility and those who have not had an adequate chance, I leave in the hands of God, knowing that He is a righteous Judge. I believe that God will provide for them in harmony with His eternal principles. We can only preach the gospel of an adequate chance. The only safe time to decide for Christ is now. This moment may be your adequate chance.

Father, nothing blocks Your redemptive grace except a stubborn will. My will is Yours. Save me today. In Jesus' name. Amen.

LAZARUS AND THE RICH MAN

FOR READING AND MEDITATION
Luke 16:19-31
- - - - - - - - - - - - - - - - - - - -
'In hell, where he was in torment,
he looked up ...' (v.23)

Hell is not a very pleasant subject to talk about, being unpopular, controversial and greatly misunderstood. However, the Bible is quite clear on the issue, and we must not shrink from facing up to what the Scriptures teach concerning hell. God doesn't send anyone to hell. The unrepentant soul sends itself, with God blocking the way at every step and reminding it by every means possible – the moral universe, the orderly creation and the message of the gospel – that to go against the will of the Creator is to consign oneself to banishment from His presence. God's commandments and moral laws are the crash barriers along the precipice of life to keep us from destroying ourselves.

O God, my Father, use my life to turn those who do not know You from their self-destruction. This I ask in Jesus' name. Amen.

SOUL SLEEP

2 Corinthians 5:1–9

'We ... would prefer to be away from the body and at home with the Lord.' (v.8)

The Bible teaches us that beyond death we shall enjoy the conscious presence of our Lord Jesus Christ. Some think the spiritual part of a Christian lapses into a comatose condition or 'soul sleep', from which he will emerge only when the last trumpet sounds. I do not believe that this is scripturally tenable. If Paul was not sure that he would consciously be in the presence of Christ immediately after death, why would he have said, 'I desire to depart and be with Christ, which is better by far' (Phil. 1:23)? He was already enjoying Christ's presence on earth. Would it be 'better by far' to leave that and go into a long state of unconscious hibernation?

Father, thank You for reminding me that to be absent from the body is to be present with the Lord. Sudden death – sudden glory.

THE SECOND COMING

WITH CHRIST IN PARADISE

Luke 23:32–43

- -

'*… today you will be with me in paradise.*' (v.43)

J esus' body was eventually placed in Joseph of Arimathea's tomb, while the body of the thief was no doubt tossed into a pauper's grave. Yet the Saviour's prediction held good: 'Today you will be with me in paradise.' The Redeemer and the repentant robber were together immediately after death, and being together would mean very little unless there was a conscious relationship. A man may be surrounded by a multitude of friends, but if he sleeps he might as well be alone. As someone has pointed out, 'Those who sleep in Jesus are not asleep to Jesus.' Sleep, when applied to death, refers only to the body, not the soul or spirit.

Father, I am so thankful that what happened to the dying thief will happen to me. I, too, shall be with You in paradise. Amen.

JOY IN THE LORD

FOR READING AND MEDITATION

Luke 15:1–10

'... there is joy in the presence of the angels of God ...' (v.10, NKJV)

Some day in the future, if Christ does not return beforehand, God will give us leave to die. What will it be like to be in our Master's presence, awaiting the final day of resurrection when our soul and body will be reunited? This blissful disembodied state will have many delights, but the one supreme thing will be everlasting joy. How often heaven and joy are linked. The heart of God Himself throbs in His being when a sinner comes to know Him. Again we hear the master say in the parable of the talents, 'Well done, good and faithful servant ... enter into the joy of your lord.'

Blessed Lord, the future is no longer a foe. It beckons because it is filled with You and Your joy. Amen.

THE MILLENNIUM – A HINGE

Revelation 20:1–6

'... *they will be priests of God and of Christ and will reign with him for a thousand years.*' (v.6)

When will Christ come again? There are three main views all hinging on today's text, which describes a reign of Christ and His people for a thousand years (ie, a millennium). One view, known as Pre-millennialism, holds that Christ will return prior to the one thousand-year reign. Another view, known as Post-millennialism, holds that the gospel will triumph throughout the world, producing a millennium of unparalleled joy, at the end of which Christ will return. A third view, known as Amillennialism, holds that the description in Revelation chapter 20 is symbolical and that it refers to the entire period of Christ's rule, beginning with His ascension. Over the coming week we shall examine each of these views.

Father, in an area where even great scholars differ, guide me, I pray, so that I see what You want me to see. Amen.

AMILLENNIALISM

Revelation 11:15–19

'The kingdom of the world has become the kingdom of our Lord ... and he will reign for ever.' (v.15)

We are in the millennium right now, say the Amillennialists. Most of them believe that the millennium is symbolical and not a literal thousand-year reign. They see the promises of the Old Testament in relation to Israel as having their fulfilment in the Christian Church – the Israel of God. Amillennialists also take the view that the first resurrection and the reign of the saints with Christ is not something that is to take place in the future but something that has taken place in the past. They see the first resurrection as either the new life a person receives when he comes to Christ (Eph. 2:5) or the victory of the martyred saints in heaven.

Father, help me to understand Your Word. Thank You that there is a time when You will reign for ever. Amen.

THE SECOND COMING

POST-MILLENNIALISM

2 Thessalonians 2:1–17

'Concerning the coming of our Lord Jesus Christ
… we ask you … not to become easily unsettled or
alarmed …' (vv.1–2)

Post-millennialists believe that Christ will return after
a one thousand-year reign of bliss and blessedness.
The Church will so influence the world by its life and
witness that kingdom principles will triumph, and thus
make the earth ready for the return of the King. Loraine
Boettner, in his book *The Millennium*, sees the task of
the Church as not simply to evangelise the world but
to Christianise it. Post-milliennialists generally see the
Church as the new Israel – the 'Israel of God' (Gal. 6:16).
Beyond all its symbols, the book of Revelation has one
basic message – God's ability to turn all things to good, and
bring about on earth the triumph of the kingdom of God.

**Father, help me not to be confused by men's views, but
to keep alive within me the fact that one day You will
return. Amen.**

'THE VALLEY OF DRY BONES'

Ezekiel 37:1–14

'... *he brought me out ... and set me in the middle of a valley; it was full of bones.*' (v.1)

Post-millennialists see in Ezekiel's vision something other than that Israel will one day be gathered together as a nation. They see, rather, a picture of the Christian Church, the 'Israel of God', being brought together bone by bone (united by the Spirit), clothed with living flesh (baptised afresh with the gifts of God), and welded together into a mighty army (empowered by the Almighty to be a strong and invincible force) that will go out into the world and make a dramatic and mighty impact for God. God's promises to ancient Israel, it is believed, are fulfilled partly in the Christian Church and partly in a spiritual turning of Jews to Christ.

Father, thank You that You can breathe life into that which to men's eyes appears to be dead. Breathe on me breath of God. Amen.

PRE-MILLENNIALISM

1 Thessalonians 4:13–18

'... *we who are still alive ... will be caught up together with them in the clouds to meet the Lord in the air.*' *(v.17)*

Pre-millennialism believes that prior to Christ's coming there will be a period of great apostasy – a falling away. Second, it believes that Jesus will come secretly for His saints and take both dead and living Christians to be with Himself – an event often referred to as 'the secret rapture' (1 Thess. 4:17). This is not the same event as His second coming to earth. It will take place in the air, prior to His coming to earth, when the saints, whether asleep or awake, will rise into a new and radiant life. They will be changed, as the Scripture says, 'in a moment, in the twinkling of an eye' (1 Cor. 15:51–52, RSV).

Father, help me now as I think again through these different and diverse views. In Jesus' name. Amen.

THE GREAT TRIBULATION

Matthew 24:14-27

'For then there will be great tribulation ...'
(v.21, RSV)

The third event in the timetable of Pre-millennialism is the period of the great tribulation on earth. Some believe that the Church will entirely escape this period of great trouble, while others think she will escape only a part of it. Finally, Christ will return to earth with His saints. This will take place at the end of the great tribulation, at which time Christ will descend to the mount from which He ascended – the Mount of Olives – whereupon He will supervise the great battle of Armageddon, and then usher in the thousand-year reign of peace and prosperity known as the millennium.

Father, help me not to be nonplussed but to pray, and there find the power to live in readiness for Your coming. Amen.

THE UNITY OF THE SPIRIT

Ephesians 4:1–13

'Make every effort to keep the unity of the Spirit through the bond of peace.' (v.3)

The final events in the timetable of Pre-millennialism are as follows: Once Christ returns to Jerusalem, He will re-establish the Temple worship and, from there, with His saints, He will rule and reign over the earth for a thousand years. After the thousand-year reign has ended, Satan, who meantime had been bound, is loosed again and will be permitted to stir up rebellion against God. He and his demons will be cast into the lake of fire and brimstone. This will be followed by the resurrection and judgment of the wicked, after which comes the final eternal state. Christians may not agree over the details of Christ's return, but we still meet and work together in the overriding unity of the Spirit.

Father, thank You that even if we cannot achieve unanimity of thought, we can still experience the unity of the Spirit. Amen.

HOW THEN SHALL WE LIVE?

2 Peter 3:11–18

'You ought to live holy and godly lives ...' (v.11)

We must not spend too much time focusing on dates, periods and signs, and so miss the whole point and purpose of the biblical references to the second coming. What is the point and purpose of such references? It is to tune our hearts to the fact that Christ is coming again and that we must be ready for that all-important event. We must not tie ourselves too rigidly to any view but, like the early Christians, look not so much for signs but for the Lord Himself. Practically every book of the New Testament bears witness to this fact – they lived as if Christ would come at any moment. And so must we!

O Father, help me live continually in the light of Your coming – eager, expectant and ready. Amen.

ALL EYES ON JESUS

FOR READING AND MEDITATION
Philippians 3:13–21

'... *we eagerly await a Saviour from there, the Lord
Jesus Christ ...*' (v.20)

My faith is not based on events, but on the Saviour.
While I am dogmatic, indeed 'bulldog-matic', on
such doctrines as the Person of Christ and the authority of
the Bible, I am aware that in relation to the actual details
of the manner of Christ's coming, it is wise to allow for
the possibility of misunderstanding. We must not allow
ourselves to become so rigidly attached to a particular
point of view on the manner of Christ's coming that we
become spiritually devastated or shattered when events
do not take place as we think they should. However we
perceive the signs of the times, we must not look for them,
but for the Saviour.

**Father, help me not to focus on signs that might
indicate the second coming but on the One to whom all
signs point – Jesus. Amen.**

LOOK UP IN EXPECTATION

FOR READING AND MEDITATION

Luke 21:25–36

'… look up … because your redemption is drawing near.' (v.28, RSV)

I t's one thing to hold the belief of the second coming in your head; it's another to let it burn in the centre of your heart like a living flame. 'Some people,' said C.S. Lewis, writing on this theme many years ago, 'find the Second Coming of Christ a difficult doctrine because it cuts across their dreams and aspirations'. Talking of those who just hoard for their future on earth, Jesus called them fools, asking 'who will get all these things you have kept for yourself?' (Luke 12:20). I ask you: Are you looking up, and eager to meet your Lord? Can you say, 'Even so, come, Lord Jesus'?

Father, help me to hold all temporal things loosely in my hands, and keep my eyes firmly fixed on eternity. Amen.

LOOK IN – EXAMINATION

1 John 3:1-10

'Everyone who has this hope in him purifies himself ...' (v.3)

The truth of Christ's second coming should cause us to live not only with an eager and expectant heart, but with a pure and exemplary life. We should always be ready for that all-important event.

Many years ago, I visited a dear old saint in the Welsh valleys, a man known throughout the whole of the principality for his love of Christ. 'What is the secret of your Christian character?' I asked him. He said, 'Ever since I was converted sixty years ago, I have tried to live before Him so that, should He come this day, I would not be ashamed at His coming.'

Father, I long so much to be pure in heart. May Christ's coming not frighten me, but inspire me to purity. Amen.

THE GREAT INTAKE

Matthew 6:24–34

'See how the lilies of the field grow.' (v.28)

We must not continually ask ourselves: Am I pure enough, holy enough, good enough to meet Christ if He were to come today? How do lilies grow? By receptivity. They take in from the soil and sun and they give back in beauty. They grow effortlessly without strain and without drain. So Jesus points us to the lilies and asks us to grow by receptivity. The struggling, nervous, overactive, pushy type of Christian, struggling to achieve more purity and holiness, is not what God wants or expects. Simply focus on Christ, rejoice in the fact that He loves you – and grow as the lilies grow, by the law of the 'Great Intake'.

Gracious Father, teach me to stop struggling, and turn everything over to You. Then receive, receive, receive – to overflowing. Amen.

LOOK OUT – IN OCCUPATION

Philemon 4–7

- - - - - - - - - - - - - - - - - - - -

'... pray that you may be active in sharing your faith ...' (v.6)

I n the light of Christ's return, we must be active in sharing our faith. However, as Doug Barnett said, 'We must stop trying to shout at people across a chasm, and start instead to build a relationship.' Isn't that the way many Christians go about sharing their faith? They shout to the unconverted from a distance rather than build the bridge of a loving relationship which would enhance the effectiveness of the message. 'A Christian,' said a theologian, 'is someone who cares.' The task of sharing our faith weighs heavily upon us, but we must remember that to share Jesus with the world means more than just the sharing of words – it means the sharing of ourselves.

**Lord Jesus, You were 'the friend of sinners'.
Help me to be like You. Amen.**

A CHRISTIAN – ONE WHO CARES

Romans 12:9–21

'Bless those who persecute you ...
Rejoice with those who rejoice ...' (vv.14–15)

I n the Andes mountains when goats meet each other
on a rocky ledge where it is difficult to pass, one will
kneel and let the other pass over him – to the safety of
both. In order to share your faith effectively, perhaps you
will have to kneel to let someone walk over you. If you
are to be a bridge between a man's indifference and his
awakening, you will be walked on. It will require deeds like
sharing people's concerns, their joys, their problems, their
sufferings. And that's costly. To try and share our faith
merely by words, without being willing to win people's
trust and earn the right to their attention, is not the pattern
set by our Master.

**Blessed Master, help me to care like You. I want to be
one who cares for people who do not care. Amen.**

AN ETERNAL PERSPECTIVE

Ephesians 1:1–12

'... *as he chose us in him before the foundation of the world ...*' (v.4, RSV)

In my view the Bible shows that behind the construction and creation of this great universe, God had in mind the selection of a Bride for His Son. This truth alone makes history comprehensible. Non-Christian historians, scientists and thinkers are just not able to conceive of a cosmos which has a love story at its heart. However, that is precisely the reason why God interrupted the flow of eternity, constructed a universe that was regulated by time and organised human life. God's desire to produce a Bride for His Son is the central theme of the universe and the goal of all that God has been doing since time began.

Father, thank You that You have chosen me to be a part of the Bride who one day will be joined to Your Son. Amen.

ALL ACCORDING TO PLAN

1 Corinthians 2:6–16

'The man without the Spirit ... cannot understand them, because they are spiritually discerned.' (v.14)

The Greeks regarded history as a complete circle, going nowhere in particular and never reaching a goal. G.N. Clark said, 'There is no secret and no plan in history to be discovered.' André Maurois, the French biographer said, 'The universe is indifferent. Who created it? Why are we here on this puny mud heap, spinning in infinite space? I have not the slightest idea and I am quite convinced no one has.' Apart from what the Bible shows us, we Christians, too, would have no idea why we are here, or what point or purpose lies behind history. However, there is no such thing as secular history. History is 'His story'. His story of finding a Bride for His Son.

Heavenly Father, thank You for reminding me again that history is really *Your* story of Your eternal plan. For Jesus' sake. Amen.

'HE DECIDED BEFOREHAND'

Acts 17:22–31

'He decided beforehand which should rise and fall, and when.' (v.26, TLB)

According to Paul, the rise and fall of great empires is in direct harmony with God's purposes and plans. Henry Halley has pointed out: 'The Old Testament is the account of a nation. The New Testament is the account of a Man. The nation was founded and nurtured by God to bring the Man into the world.' Though many cannot see it at the moment, the day will come when the whole universe will recognise that the events which have taken place over the long history of earth's ages have been ordered, directed and supervised by God with one glorious end in view – the wooing and winning of a Bride for His eternal Son.

Father, thank You for Your infinite wisdom and ability and that even I am part of Your plans. Thank You, Father. Amen.

WHERE HISTORY BEGINS

FOR READING AND MEDITATION
Revelation 13:1–8

'... the Lamb that was slain from the creation of the world.' (v.8)

The text before us today reveals the thrilling truth that God had a Lamb before He had a Man. When God laid down the broad beams of creation in the distant ages of the past, He made the cross an integral part of the universe. Christian teachers have always insisted that Christ was once offered for sins and that Calvary is a fact of recorded time. With this there can be no disagreement, but we must also see that before there was a cross raised on Calvary, there was a cross built into the universe from the very foundation of the world. That is the point at which history begins.

Father, You built Your universe on a cross. When You planned the cosmos, You had my eternal salvation in mind. I am so grateful. Amen.

THE SECOND COMING

THE TRIUMPH OF THE AGES

John 10:11–18

'… I lay down my life … No one takes it from me, but I lay it down of my own accord.' (vv.17–18)

When Adam sinned in the beginning, being the representative of the human race that was to follow, he handed over the title deeds of humanity, so to speak, to the devil. Christ, being the representative of a new order of humanity, was able by His death to redeem men and women and open up to them the potential of transferring their allegiance from Satan to God. At the cross, therefore, Satan lost his legal rights to the title deeds of humanity and now all those who by an act of free will commit themselves to Jesus Christ, are delivered from the bondage of sin and Satan, and are made heirs of God and joint heirs with Christ.

Father, the cross is not only the centre of the universe, it is central in my life, too. Thank You, Father. Amen.

A FULL DRESS REHEARSAL

Genesis 2:21–25; John 19:32–34

'... and while he slept took one of his ribs ...'
(Gen. 2:21, RSV)

Why didn't God make Eve out of dust like Adam?
I believe it is a picture of Christ and His Bride the
Church. Both Eve and the Church were created from one
body and then joined by God so that the two become one.
In the act of human creation, you have a perfect picture
of what God designed for His Son. On the cross God took
from the body of the Lord Jesus Christ the element of
blood, and in that blood He washes all those who in simple
faith surrender to Him. At the cross a new humanity is
created – a company of blood-washed people who will one
day be married to Christ in eternity.

**Father, thank You that I have been chosen to be a part
of the Bride who will be joined to Your Son. Amen.**

THE SECOND COMING

THE GOAL OF THE UNIVERSE

Ephesians 1:1–14

'… he purposed long ago … that all human history should be consummated in Christ, that everything … should find its perfection and fulfillment in him.'
(v.10, Phillips)

Genesis 5:2 says, 'He created them male and female and blessed them … he called them [plural] "man" [singular].' Notice what it says, 'He called them "man".' I take this to mean that God put the woman in the man, then later took her out of the man and then joined her yet again to him, to become bone of his bone and flesh of his flesh. Here, as I said yesterday, God is laying down a truth that later He wants to reveal in greater perspective, namely that the Church, the Bride of Christ, was actually in Christ in eternity, taken out of Him in time, and will be joined together again with Him in the eternity that is to come.

Father, I am so glad that You included me in Your most marvellous purpose. Thank You, Father. Amen.

A ROYAL WEDDING

FOR READING AND MEDITATION
Revelation 19:1–9

'For the wedding of the Lamb has come,
and his bride has made herself ready.' (v.7)

Although, as Christians, we may disagree on the various aspects of Christ's coming, we all agree on the fact that the final destiny of the Church is to be joined with Christ for ever. We are destined for a royal wedding. The Scripture sets the scene for the espousal in heaven. Hallelujahs roll like thunder around the throne. Then comes the official announcement: 'Let us rejoice and be glad and give him glory! For the wedding of the Lamb has come, and his bride has made herself ready.' The wedding between Christ and the Church will be the greatest and most spectacular the universe has ever witnessed or seen.

Father, I know I shall be present at that wedding.
And not only present, but part of it. Hallelujah! Amen.

ONE WITH HIM

Ephesians 5:21–32

'... and the two will become one ... I am talking about Christ and the church.' (vv.31–32)

Paul says of this marriage union between Christ and His Church: 'The two shall become one ... This is a great mystery, but I speak concerning Christ and the church (NKJV).' Just reflect on that for a moment. What is the 'great mystery'? This: when Christ comes to take us to be with Himself, He is not going to transform us into angelic beings – He is going to make us one with Himself. We shall be made like Him – a perfect partner for the perfect Bridegroom. What a prospect. The destiny awaiting us is not that of becoming angelic beings or any other type of celestial being. We shall be one with our Saviour – for ever!

Jesus, just to be near You in eternity would be sufficient, but to be one with You is a prospect that utterly overwhelms me. Amen.

ON THE EDGE OF ETERNITY

1 Corinthians 15:20–28

'Then the end will come … after he has destroyed all dominion, authority and power.' (v.24)

There will be an end of sin and pain, but the end will really be a new beginning. A small blind girl had her sight restored. When the bandages were removed, the girl looked out at the beauty of the world and said, 'Oh, Mummy, why didn't you tell me it was as lovely as this.' Brushing away her tears, the mother said, 'My darling, I did my best to tell you but there were just not enough words to describe it. You had to see it for yourself.' Similarly, the delights and wonders of eternity are ultimately indescribable. But one day we will see it for ourselves.

O Father, what a future, what a hope, what a glorious eternity. Even so, come, Lord Jesus! Amen.

THE SECOND COMING

AT-ONEMENT

FOR READING AND MEDITATION
Romans 5:1–11

'... *our Lord Jesus Christ, by whom we have now
received the atonement.' (v.11, AV)*

William Tyndale, when translating the Bible into
English, joined two words together – 'at' and
'onement' and this has been accepted by theologians down
the centuries as the official technical term for the doctrine
of Christ's substitutionary death on the cross. Through the
cross we become at one with God. The word pictures two
estranged parties being brought together. This is precisely
what Christ's atoning death achieved – it brought a holy
God into a new relationship with sinful man, and made
it potentially possible for both to live together in perfect
harmony and peace. Modern translations use the word
'reconciliation', but the thought is the same in describing
the redeeming work of the Lord Jesus Christ.

**Father, make the atonement more than a doctrine in my
mind – let it be a delight in my heart. Amen.**

SIN – A UNIVERSAL FACT

Psalm 14:1–7

'... *all have strayed away; all are rotten with sin.*'
(v.3, TLB)

The need for the atonement is because of: (1) the widespread influence of sin, (2) the seriousness of sin and (3) man's utter inability to atone for himself. Every human being is a sinner – the one exception being the Lord Jesus Christ. Sin is a universal fact affecting every person, irrespective of race, class or colour. I realise that some people take strong exception to being called a sinner, and insist we need a new word to describe our human plight – a new but less sinister word. What we really need, however, is not a new word for sin but a new understanding of the word we already have.

O Father, help me to realise that when I sin, I am a sinner and in need of the atonement through Jesus Christ. Amen.

THE CONTRADICTION OF GOD

Psalm 51:1–13

'Against you, you only, have I sinned ... (v.4)

The most common word for sin is the Greek word *hamartia* which means 'missing the mark'. There is a mark, a standard, written into the fabric of the universe, and all departure from that is sin. And what is this mark, this standard? It is the character of God. When we fail to live according to God's character we 'miss the mark' and, by reason of this, we are sinners. When Scripture says that 'sin is the transgression of the law' (1 John 3:4), it must be seen that the law is the transcript of God's character. The awful thing about sin is not so much that we break God's law but that we break His heart.

Father, breaking Your laws wounds Your own dear heart. Keep me from sin. In Jesus' name I ask it. Amen.

THE SERIOUSNESS OF SIN

Habakkuk 1:12–17

'... *you, who cannot allow sin in any form ...*'
(*v.13, TLB*)

Sin separates man from God (Isa. 59:2). And for
those who die unrepentant, never experiencing
the forgiveness of their sins, there remains 'a fearful
expectation of judgment and of raging fire' (Heb. 10:27).
This age has polluted the very language by which we
communicate. Lies are called fibs. Stealing is called
scrounging. Homosexual relationships are called 'gay'
experiences. Pre-marital or extra-marital sex is called
'love', when the real word is 'lust'. Sin is sin, even if we
call it by other names. Nobody can ever understand the
atonement of Christ, or God's plan for the world, until he
or she learns to recognise sin for what it is, and to view it in
its proper light.

**Father, help me to evaluate everything not simply by
the standards of society, but under the searching light
of Scripture. Amen.**

THE ATONEMENT

POISON OR PEPPERMINT?

FOR READING AND MEDITATION
Proverbs 15:20–33

'The LORD is far from the wicked ...' (v.29)

A deacon asked a minister not to talk about sin but about mistakes and errors. The minister walked over to a cupboard and took a bottle marked 'Poison'. 'What would you say,' he asked the deacon, 'if I removed the label marked "Poison" and replaced it with a label marked "Peppermint"?' 'Why,' said the deacon, 'that would be a very dangerous thing to do.' 'Exactly,' said the minister, 'and it is equally dangerous to tamper with the labels which God has put on certain issues. Sin is sin is sin.'

You don't make a deadly thing innocuous by giving it a different name. Appendicitis is still appendicitis even when you call it a bit of indigestion.

Father, impress deep upon my spirit the solemnity and seriousness of sin, that I might not take it lightly. Amen.

TOTAL DEPRAVITY

Proverbs 20:1–9

'Who can say, "I have made my heart pure;
I am clean and without sin?"' (v.9)

Theologians refer to 'the doctrine of total depravity' meaning that man is totally incapable of earning his own salvation, and utterly powerless to do for himself what needs to be done. Does this mean that man is incapable of performing any act of kindness? In my judgment the doctrine of total depravity does not set out to dismiss or deny the fact that a certain amount of goodness resides in the human heart. What it attempts to set forth is the fact that goodness cannot save man. Man has many natural virtues, and we cannot shut our eyes to that fact, but those virtues, good though they may be, are insufficient to merit a man's acceptance with God.

Father, I see so clearly that You had to condemn me before You could save me. Thank You, Father. Amen.

SO GOOD – YET SO BAD

Mark 10:17–27

'Jesus looked at him and loved him … He went away sad, because he had great wealth.' (vv.21–22)

D id the rich young ruler love the Lord with all his heart? Hardly – because he would not follow Him. What about loving his neighbour as himself? Had he kept that commandment? No. Because if he had, he would not for an instant have hesitated at Christ's invitation to bestow his goods upon the poor. Who can deny that, for all his virtues, the rich young ruler cuts a very sorry figure indeed, and that his natural goodness, undeniable though it was, was not good enough. Let it be said, and said with great force, that no one is capable of saving himself. 'The Lord must save and He alone' should ever remain the watchword of our evangelical faith.

O God, my Father, help me to take Your way in everything – whatever the cost. In Jesus' name. Amen.

GOD'S RECOVERY PROGRAMME

Hebrews 11:1–10, 39–12:3

'God had planned something better for us ...' (11:40)

hristianity has been defined as 'the divine recovery programme' – God doing for man what he couldn't do for himself. The 'recovery plan' begins to appear, in outline form at least, in the pages of the Old Testament. It spells out in different ways and in different forms the awesome truth that atonement can only be provided through a substitutionary sacrifice. In the Old Testament we see the offering of Isaac and the substitution of a ram, the brass serpent, the Tabernacle, priests and sacrifices. However, there was something better to come, no, *Someone* better – the One who makes full atonement for the sins of the world.

Father, how exciting the Old Testament becomes when I view it as the beginning of Your glorious 'recovery plan'. I see Christ everywhere. Amen.

GOD'S REQUIREMENT

FOR READING AND MEDITATION
Luke 17:11–19

'When he saw them, he said, "Go, show yourselves to the priests." And as they went, they were cleansed.' (v.14)

If an animal was used for sacrifice it had to be as unblemished and as perfect as possible. Theoretically it had to be the utmost for the highest. God wanted to lay deep down in human consciousness the fact that atonement can only be effected through a perfect sacrifice. In point of fact, some Israelites, outwardly religious but grudging in their hearts, would offer an imperfect sacrifice – a lamb that was ailing, a pair of scruffy pigeons or a defective dove which they had bought cheaply. How sad that what should have been the utmost for the highest turned out so often to be the least for the highest.

Father, help me to be a maximum Christian – one who gives the utmost, not the least, for the highest. In Jesus' name I pray. Amen.

WHOLLY PURE

Exodus 28:36–43

'... *[Aaron] will bear the guilt involved in the sacred gifts ...' (v.38)*

Are we, in this modern age, guilty of iniquity in holy things? I think we are. Sometimes our repentance is merely remorse at being found out. How much of our Christian activity is performed out of the itch for praise or the covert bid for admiration? Do we give to be seen of men? Do we indulge ourselves and bring to God's altar less than we should – and grudgingly at that? Aaron bore the guilt of impure sacrifices. Now one greater than Aaron comes to our aid. Christ, the heavenly Mediator, will save us not only from our vices but from our 'virtues' too!

Father, I sometimes offer the lowest as the highest. Cleanse me from all sin and condemnation and make me wholly pure. In Jesus' name. Amen.

'NOT TO BE TAKEN LIGHTLY'

Leviticus 1:1–9

'... he shall offer a male without blemish ... that he may be accepted before the LORD ...' (v.3, RSV)

I n order to worship God and have his sins forgiven, a man was obliged to bring to the priest an animal which had to be his rightful property. The sacrificer placed his hands upon the head of the offering while stating the reason for his sacrifice (Lev. 1:3; 4:4). It was as though the person put away sin from himself and transferred it to the body of the helpless animal. In most private offerings, the person killed his own sacrifice. Atonement is not cheap, and God, by insisting on painstaking ritual and a valuable sacrifice, laid down the principle that sin is never to be taken lightly.

Father, I look beyond this Old Testament picture to Calvary, and see in wonder there what it cost You to provide atonement for my sin.

ONE FOR ANOTHER

Leviticus 22:17–33

'I am the LORD, who makes you holy ...' (v.32)

In the shed blood of the animal, the life was poured out to bring about death – nothing more could man give, and nothing less could God accept. After the blood was applied to the altar, portions of the flesh of some offerings could be eaten while other parts were burned on the altar. Does it not now become apparent how our Lord's sacrifice on Calvary is reflected in the blood-red altars of Israel? Can you not see how His blameless life, His violent death – the nailing of His body to the cross – even the way He offered His soul to God, is the fulfilment of all that went before? Hallelujah – what a Saviour!

Lord Jesus, I gaze on Your surpassing worth and my heart melts with gratitude and praise. I want nothing other than You. Amen.

THE DAY OF ATONEMENT

Leviticus 16:6–22

'... and bring its blood within the veil ...
thus he shall make atonement ...' (vv.15–16, RSV)

The Day of Atonement was an annual ritual when there were sacrifices for sin. The priest would make offerings for the whole nation in the Holy of Holies, sprinkling blood before the mercy seat in the Tabernacle. Eventually, the high priest came out, walked over to the scapegoat, which during the service had stood before the congregation, and confessed over it the sins of the people, after which the goat was led away into the wilderness to be released in a desolate place. Next he would kill the goat that had not been chosen to be the scapegoat, and entering into the Holy of Holies would sprinkle the blood as before.

Father, I am so thankful that Christ is the final sacrifice for my sins and that through His blood I have obtained mercy. Amen.

REMOVED — OR COVERED?

Romans 3:21–31

'... *in his forbearance he had left the sins committed beforehand unpunished – he did it to demonstrate his justice* ...' (vv.25–26)

Old Testament sacrifices 'covered' the offerer's sin, and as his offering implied confession, it also secured his forgiveness. It was only the sacrifice of Christ that actually removed sins and made us totally at one with God. This is what Paul is bringing out in the passage before us today, I believe: 'For he was looking forward to the time when Christ would come and take away those sins' (v.25, TLB). Clearly then, the word 'atonement' in the Old Testament doesn't carry the force it has in the New, for only Christ's sacrifice can truly bring a man or woman into at-onement with God.

O Father, I am so thankful that I am at-one with You. I am redeemed, reconciled and rejoicing. Thank You, Father. Amen.

JESUS IS THE ATONEMENT

FOR READING AND MEDITATION

John 1:29–34

'Behold, the Lamb of God, who takes away the sin of the world!' (v.29, RSV)

Dr Edwards of Bala wrote: 'This is the Atonement – not the sufferings and not the death but the Person of the Son of God in the sufferings and the death. It is not that He made the Atonement, or paid the Atonement. The Bible goes far beyond that. He is the Atonement – not He Himself without the act, but He Himself in the act.' Jesus, while never ceasing to be what He had always been (true God), became what He had never been before (true Man). If Christ is to be our representative, He can only be so if He is really part of the human race. Our Saviour, therefore, gave Himself *to* us before He gave Himself *for* us.

Lord, help me to see that if You had failed to give Yourself *to* me then You could not have given Yourself *for* me. Amen.

THE MAN — CHRIST JESUS

1 Timothy 2:1–6

- -

'For there is one God and one mediator between God and men, the man Christ Jesus ...' (v.5)

When Jesus Christ became Man, He became a truly human person. He took to Himself a human soul as well as a human body, and His Spirit, which was part of the Godhead, became the driving force of His personality, enabling Him to function as the God-Man. This combination of two natures in one personality is the supreme miracle of the ages. Jesus entered into the experience of human psychical life as well as of human physical life. His manhood was complete. But what is more, it is permanent. Though now exalted, He continues to be God and Man, one Person for ever.

Jesus, I stand in awe before the wonder of Your incarnation. I cannot probe its mystery but I can enter into all its benefits. Amen.

THE ATONEMENT

THE IMMACULATE CONCEPTION

Luke 1:26–38

'You will … give birth to a son, and you are to give him the name Jesus.' (v.31)

Why was it necessary for Christ to be born of a virgin, and why did He have to come into the world that way? His conception was brought about, not in the usual way by the joining of a male sperm with a female egg, but by the direct energy of the Holy Spirit within the womb of Mary. This meant two things: (1) a miraculous conception ensured that He would be born without the natural human bias toward sin, and (2) the replacement in His conception of the male principle by the Holy Spirit of God meant that something utterly without parallel took place – God and humanity were miraculously blended in one personality.

O Jesus, Redeemer and Lord, how grateful I am for Your incarnation. You became like me, so that I could become like You. Amen.

THE IMPECCABLE CHRIST

John 7:12; 8:42–51

'Which of you convicts me of sin?' (8:46, RSV)

Jesus was not only born without original sin, He lived a sinless life. Doubtless it is the mark of a good person that he has a keen sense of guilt. Yet here in our text today, Jesus, who, as most people admit was a good man, makes the challenging statement: 'Which of you convicts me of sin?' He had no personal sin, and, what was more, those who lived with Him intimately, such as His disciples, and who saw Him in all kinds of situations, did not take up this challenge. They did not because they could not. He was not just good – He was perfect.

Jesus, thank You that You were without sin, and so you are the perfect substitute and can bear my sins before God. Amen.

TEMPTED – LIKE WE ARE

Matthew 4:1–11

'Then Jesus was led by the Spirit into the desert to be tempted by the devil.' (v.1)

Jesus was not shielded from the hurts and weaknesses which are common to the human condition but He was '… tempted in every way, just as we are – yet was without sin' (Heb. 4:15). He, like us, had to resist temptation in order to overcome it.

A soldier offered a starving little girl a bite of his sandwich. Her mind had been so affected by propaganda that she refused it – it might be poisoned. The serviceman took a bite of the sandwich and said, 'I take a bite – you take a bite.' She finished the sandwich. Jesus not only tasted death for every man, He tasted life with every man. He asks us to do nothing that He Himself would not do.

Jesus, You did not live apart from humanity or above humanity, but alongside humanity. You identified with us in everything – except sin. Amen.

LONELINESS

John 6:52–66

'At this point many of his disciples turned away and deserted him.' (v.66, TLB)

There were many times in Jesus' life when He must have felt lonely. Some disciples deserted Him, while His closest friends ran away and denied Him. He was not bereft of His Father's presence for one single moment, but being human as well as divine, He would have longed for human companionship. Jesus had no home. Look at the last verse of John chapter 7 and the first verse of John chapter 8. It is really one verse. The chapter division comes in the wrong place. 'Then each went to his own home. But Jesus went to the Mount of Olives.' Everyone had his own house to go to. Everyone – except the Son of God.

Lord, You speak to my condition because You have been in my condition. I am so thankful. I feel Your comforting presence. Amen.

THE ATONEMENT

HE WEPT

Luke 19:37–48

'As he approached Jerusalem and saw the city, he wept over it ...' (v.41)

Perhaps nothing proves Jesus' humanity more than His ability to weep. Jesus was not afraid to let people see Him with tears in His eyes. Jesus knew how to feel His emotions, and demonstrated to those around the fact that He was fully human as well as fully divine. He has gone through everything I have gone through. Men, in manufacturing their gods out of their imagination, had to make their gods so strong that they would never weep. If they did, they would betray their earthliness. But Jesus wept! And, in doing so, betrayed the fact that He was, indeed, well and truly one of us.

Blessed Redeemer, You have the marks of my humanity upon You and through them I see the deeper mystery that You are God. Amen.

THE SHADOW OF THE CROSS

John 3:1–17

'Just as Moses lifted up the snake in the desert,
so the Son of Man must be lifted up ...' (v.14)

How conscious was our Lord of His impending death? Early in His ministry, Jesus explained that for us to be born again, the Son of God must die. His incarnation is not enough. His miracles are not enough. His ministry is not enough. He must die! It was a snake that made the Israelites ill and it was a snake that made them well. Whoever looked at the snake would live (Num. 21:6–9). Here we see a glimpse of a truth that Paul later enlarged upon when he said, 'God made him who had no sin to be sin for us ...' (2 Cor. 5:21). Christ became our sin in order that He may become our salvation.

Jesus, I sense today how heavily the shadow of the cross must have fallen upon You. Thank You for going through with it for me. Amen.

THE ATONEMENT

THE PASSOVER LAMB

John 6:25–51

- - - - - - - - - - - - - - - - - - - -

'This bread is my flesh, which I will give for the life of the world.' (v.51)

The annual Jewish Passover Feast was near (John 6:4). On the Passover, the blood of the lamb was sprinkled on the doorposts of houses and each family ate the flesh (Exod. 12:8–11). Was it this thought that prompted Jesus to make the statement He did? He was truly the Passover Lamb. His death would avert the terror of sin's terrifying judgment, eternal death, and His flesh would give new life and strength to those who would receive Him and follow Him. The full meaning of these words was not understood by the people, or even by the disciples, but in His own heart, our Lord saw quite clearly the event awaiting Him at Golgotha.

Jesus, I see the pain You bore even before those nails of the cross were hammered into Your hands. And I love You. Amen.

THE COMING OF THE GREEKS

John 12:20–33

- -

'Now there were some Greeks among those who went up to worship at the Feast.' (v.20)

When Jesus heard that some Gentiles had come to see Him, we read that His soul was troubled. I believe the issue facing Christ was this – Athens or Jerusalem. A philosopher's chair or a grisly cross? Jesus knew that the Jews would reject Him and that through that rejection, which would culminate on a cross, the offer of salvation would be widened to take in the Gentiles. The statement He made immediately following their visit would seem to indicate that this was so: 'But I, when I am lifted up from the earth, will draw all men to myself.' Our Lord knew that He must die if all men are to be brought to Him.

Blessed Lord Jesus, You bore the agony of Your anticipated death, not for Your own benefit, but for mine. Thank You, Lord Jesus. Amen.

THE ATONEMENT

A DEATH WISH?

Luke 12:49–59

'But I have a baptism to undergo, and how distressed I am until it is completed!' (v.50)

In the passage before us today, approximately one year before His death on the cross, Jesus talks of it in such a way as if He is eager to get to grips with it. Was this, as some have suggested, a death wish? No. A death wish is a subconscious desire to die, usually as the result of deep feelings of inner guilt. But Jesus had no guilt; He was sinless, spotless and free from any moral stain. His desire to get to grips with the cross was born not out of a concern to atone for His own sin (for He had no sin), but to bear the punishment for your sin and mine.

Jesus, I shall be grateful to You for all eternity for being so willing to carry my sins to Calvary. There You bore them all away. Amen.

MARCH 26
IT SHOWED ON HIS FACE!

FOR READING AND MEDITATION

Luke 9:51–56

'… his face was set for the journey to Jerusalem.'
(v.53, NKJV)

We will never be able to plumb the full meaning of this strange statement, but it does help us, in a small way perhaps, to understand something of the awful pain that Christ was carrying in His heart – pain that in some strange way revealed itself on His face. It was not the physical act of dying that tore His soul apart, but the fact that He was about to bear the consummate guilt and wickedness of the whole human race. Never has a human heart carried such a burden and borne such a load. And His determination and agony showed up on His face.

Blessed Master, help me I pray, to become a more sensitive person to the pains others carry. For Your own dear name's sake. Amen.

THE ATONEMENT

A MOMENT OF COMFORT

FOR READING AND MEDITATION

Mark 14:1–9

'She poured perfume on my body beforehand to prepare for my burial.' (v.8)

Jesus knew He was going to die, but experienced a moment of great comfort. Traditionally, such expensive perfume was kept to anoint a person's body after death, but Mary (who we believe this was, see John 12:3) was determined to lavish it upon Him now – while He was alive. After His death, women took sweet spices for the purpose of anointing His body. However, they failed in their objective because when they got to the tomb, His body was not there! He was no longer dead but radiantly alive. Mary of Bethany, it appears, with an incredible sense of timing, recognised that if she didn't give a practical demonstration of her love for Jesus then, she might never have another opportunity.

Father, help me to be alert to every opportunity to demonstrate my love for You. Amen.

A BIBLICAL CAMEO

FOR READING AND MEDITATION

John 12:23–36

*'… it was for this very reason I came
to this hour.' (v.27)*

Jesus referred to His impending death many times.
At the first Passover, He spoke of the destruction
of His body and that He would become the new Temple
(John 2:19–21). After Peter's confession He explained His
suffering to come in Jerusalem (Matt. 16:21). Following the
transfiguration Jesus spoke of His resurrection (Mark 9:9).
When He described Himself as the Good Shepherd, He
repeated no less than three times that He was going to lay
down His life for His sheep. These statements (and many
more) indicate that the thought of His atoning death was
constantly in His mind, and during His ministry, He lived
almost always under its shadow.

**Blessed Jesus, thank You for giving me a glimpse of
Your own consciousness of Your impending death on
the cross for me. Amen.**

THE ATONEMENT

PROPITIATION

FOR READING AND MEDITATION

1 John 4:7–18

'... he loved us and sent his Son to be the propitiation for our sins.' (v.10, NKJV)

Understanding New Testament words will deepen our comprehension of the atonement. Propitiation (modern translations read 'atoning sacrifice') means to conciliate, to appease or to placate one's anger. The anger of God against sin is something about which we hear very little. God is love, but He can also be angry. Do not confuse anger with hate. If I love my child I will be angry at everything which might hurt him. I will take a serious view of anything which might seek to destroy him morally, physically or spiritually. God is angry against anything that will hurt me or demean me, but He has made a way of condemning the sin and forgiving the sinner.

Father, through the cross You have expressed Your anger against sin and Your love for the sinner. Thank You, Father. Amen.

RECONCILIATION

2 Corinthians 5:11–21

'All this is from God, who reconciled us to himself through Christ ...' (v.18)

Reconciliation means to cause or effect a thorough change. Reconciliation applies to the doing away of enmity, the bridging over of a quarrel. The way to overcome the enmity created by a quarrel is to remove the cause of the quarrel. An apology has to be made, money may have to be paid or some form of restitution effected. The way to reconciliation is through an effective grappling with the root cause of the enmity. Christ died in order to put away our sin, and on the cross He dealt with the enmity that existed between God and man. Reconciliation brings about in the believing sinner a thorough change towards God from enmity to love, confidence and trust.

Father, You have reached out to me across the chasm that divided us, and have reconciled me to Yourself through Your beloved Son. Amen.

REDEMPTION

Ephesians 1:1–12

----

*'In him we have redemption
through his blood ...' (v.7)*

Redemption means the deliverance from some evil
by the payment of a corresponding price. The term
is related closely to slavery and the slave markets, which
were so prolific in New Testament times. The Bible often
pictures sinners as being slaves, for they are gripped,
seized and manacled by the awful power of evil from
which they cannot extricate themselves. If they are to be
set free then someone else has to pay a corresponding
price. Two thousand years ago, Jesus Christ walked
into the slave market of sin and through His death and
sufferings on the cross, put down the price needed for
humanity to be set free.

**Father, I realise that I am redeemed from sin in order
to experience Your freedom in everything I do. I am
eternally grateful. Amen.**

FORGIVENESS

Colossians 1:1–14

'... in whom we have redemption, the forgiveness of sins.' (v.14)

The word 'forgive' implies that an atonement has been made and the person offering the sacrifice is now set free from guilt and blame. God's forgiveness is made possible through the redemption which is 'through his blood' (v.14, NKJV). God forgives, but it is not a cheap forgiveness. It cost God to forgive. The cross is the price God paid to get to us in spite of our sin. Divine forgiveness takes upon itself the pain, the hurt and the shame of the one forgiven. In a sense this is what we do, too, when we forgive. We take a hurt, bear it in our soul and respond by a free and full forgiveness. It costs to forgive.

O God, help me to forgive others as You have forgiven me. Let forgiveness not just be a principle but a practice. Amen.

THE ATONEMENT

JUSTIFICATION

Romans 3:19–26

'... justified freely by his grace ...' (v.24)

Justification means 'standing in the presence of God just as if one had never sinned'. To Paul, justification is an act of God by which He remits the sins of guilty men and women, and through their faith in Jesus Christ, regards them as righteous. God, in taking this action, is perfectly just because Jesus, acting on their behalf, has satisfied the claims of God's laws upon them. Paul says in Romans 5:21 that 'grace reigns through righteousness'. He does not say that grace reigns over righteousness – this would mean that God could attempt to forgive us without an atonement. That would not work because God cannot be untrue to His nature. We are justified freely at great cost.

O God, I am lost in wonder, love and praise as I stand before You as if I had never sinned. What amazing grace. Amen.

ADOPTION

Galatians 3:26–4:7

'... that we might receive the adoption as sons.'
(4:5, NKJV)

The English word 'adoption' comes from a Greek word, the literal meaning of which is 'placing as a son'. Adoption is not a word that defines a relationship but a word that defines a position. A Christian's relationship to God comes from the new birth, whereas adoption is the act of God by which He establishes us in His kingdom as an adult son. This is a word which looks at a believer's position from God's perspective, and tells us that as far as God is concerned, we are His adopted children, possessing all the family rights, including access to the Father, as well as having a share in Christ's great inheritance (Rom. 8:15, 17).

Father, I'm grateful that I am an adopted son of God. I, a child of the dust, am now a child of God. Amen.

THE ATONEMENT

SALVATION

Hebrews 2:1–15

- -

'... *how shall we escape if we ignore such a great salvation?*' (v.3)

T he word 'salvation' has a wide meaning, but basically it means deliverance or preservation from danger and difficulty, and implies safety, health and prosperity. To receive salvation in the biblical sense is to be remade in Christ, or to be in the process of that great change. The Bible talks about the penalty, the power and the presence of sin, and so the term continually grows in meaning. We are saved from the penalty of sin, we are being saved from the power of sin and we will ultimately be saved from the presence of sin. The word 'salvation' has to be interpreted very much by its context.

O Father, help me to experience not just salvation, but full salvation. In Jesus' name I pray. Amen.

DO I NEED TO UNDERSTAND IT?

FOR READING AND MEDITATION
1 Corinthians 1:18–31

'For the message of the cross is foolishness to those who are perishing, but to us who are being saved it is the power of God.' (v.18)

We do not need to understand the various theories about the cross in order to be saved by it. The cross works for the most illiterate and uneducated person, providing they reach out in simple faith and appropriate its power. One's inability to comprehend or explain how the death of Christ atones for the soul makes no difference to its power to save, providing, as I said, one knows how to lay hold of it in simple faith. Electricity works for all of us even though only a few understand the technicalities of it. So it is with the cross. It can work for those who do not understand, so long as they trust themselves to it.

Father, thank You that although I am unable to fathom all the mystery of the cross, I can still avail myself of its saving power. Amen.

THE ATONEMENT

'FOR ME'

1 Corinthians 15:20–28

'For as in Adam all die, so in Christ all will be made alive.' (v.22)

Some ask: how can Christ's death on the cross save me now when it took place 2,000 years ago? Have you ever had an operation in which an anaesthetic was used? Although anaesthetic was discovered before you were born, it was discovered for you. You can benefit from it now. It would be pointless to argue and say, 'No, it was not for me, it was for someone else.' Sir James Simpson could not foresee your existence in the world when he discovered chloroform, but you can say with truth when about to undergo an operation: 'It was for me, for me.' In the same way, Christ's death on the cross was for you. It avails for you.

Jesus, thank You for showing me that even before I was born, You had provided for my salvation. 'It was for me, for me.' Amen.

'I DID THAT'

Matthew 27:11–31

----

*'All the people answered, "Let his blood be on us
and on our children!"' (v.25)*

Another question asked is this: how can my sins be
atoned for by Jesus when He actually died centuries
before I committed any? A certain Negro spiritual has
a verse that says: 'I was there when they crucified my
Lord.' In what sense can it be said that you and I were
there at the cross when Jesus died? We were represented
there – represented by the people who were involved
and implicated in the death of our Lord. Many of them
were ordinary people like you and me. But, like you and
me, they refused to accept God's way for their lives and
determined to live without Him. You were represented at
the cross.

**Jesus, I was represented at Calvary just as if my own
hands had hammered in the nails, yet, You love and
forgive me. Amen.**

IT HAD TO BE

Luke 24:13–35

'Did not the Christ have to suffer these things and then enter his glory?' (v.26)

God couldn't find a way to forgive without the cross. There was no way that sin could be forgiven except by a divine atonement. God cannot do anything. He cannot, for example, make a square circle. God cannot deny His own nature – be vindictive, evil or unkind. God cannot forgive sin without the cross because the consequence of sin (not just the punishment of it) is death. The human race is so infected with the dread disease called sin that there is nothing anyone can do about it. It had to be exposed at Calvary and have its evil power destroyed by the death of the Son of God.

Lord, thank You for showing me once again the necessity for the cross. A great crime – a great love. Thank You, Lord Jesus. Amen.

SIN CRUCIFIES GOD

FOR READING AND MEDITATION
Matthew 27:33–50

'And sitting down, they kept watch over him there.' (v.36)

I t was necessary for Christ to die such a violent death that He could fully expose sin. Have you ever seen the germs which cause disease under a microscope? The things that look so innocent, harmless and even beautiful, destroy human features, eat a person's living flesh away and bring them down into the most horrible of deaths. You didn't realise the deadly character of the germ when you looked at it under a microscope, but when you see what it does, you come away with a different impression. So it is with sin. Stand at the cross and see what it does. It does that. There sin is seen in all its hideous foulness. A crucified Saviour reveals it.

Lord, if my sin did that to You then how can I sin again? Lord, keep me from sinning. Amen.

THE ATONEMENT

A CERTIFIED DEATH

John 19:28–37

'With that, he bowed his head and gave up his spirit.' (v.30)

Christ was put to death by representatives from all parts of society. God's high priest applied for it and the people themselves agreed to it. It was the deed of the nation, and accomplished officially and publicly. But His death had to be more than violent and official – it had to be certified. So that there could be no argument about the fact that He did die, and not just swoon, on the cross, it was necessary for His death to be confirmed by the authorities. And confirm it they did. 'Make sure He is dead,' said the Jews, 'and clear the crosses, for it is our great feast.' 'He is dead,' said the Romans.

Lord Jesus, I thank You again for being willing to bear my sins and die for me as a divine atonement. Amen.

BACK FROM THE DEAD

FOR READING AND MEDITATION

Mark 16:1–8

'He has risen! He is not here.' (v.6)

The crucifixion and the resurrection are really all one piece. The Victor of death was to come back from the dead to validate His claims. Because Christ's death was a certified death this meant that it was undeniable. He also had to have an undeniable resurrection. This is no half-crucified Saviour who walks out of the tomb on the resurrection morning. He is the One who suffered the excruciating agonies of the cross, passed through the portals of death, descended into Hades and then, on the third day, turned the tables on Satan and his minions by coming back from the dead, and offering to all who believe the benefits of His great atoning death.

O risen, glorified Lord, I rejoice not only because You are alive, but because I am alive in You. Hallelujah! Amen.

THE ATONEMENT

OMPTED THE
NT?

Romans 5:1–11

'But God shows his love for us in that while we were yet sinners Christ died for us.' (v.8, RSV)

What motivated God to provide the atonement? Was it justice? Was it righteousness? Was it honour? Or was it love? Some Christians suggest the atonement originated in the righteousness of God to restore balance. Others have said that the atonement originated in the justice of God because He must punish sin. The real truth, in my view, is that God, in providing the atonement, was not motivated primarily by His righteousness, His honour or His justice, but by His love. One hymnist wrote: 'Love led Him to die, And on this we rely. He hath loved, He hath loved us. We cannot tell why.'

Father, when I feel Your pulse of love, I feel Your heartbeat. Teach me more, dear Lord. For Jesus' sake. Amen.

GOD LOVES YOU

Ephesians 2:1–10

'But because of his great love for us, God, who is rich in mercy, made us alive with Christ ...' (vv.4–5)

od's holiness is what He stands for; God's righteousness is what He does; God's justice is what He demands; God's love is what He is. It is love that balances all God's attributes. Justice and holiness would send us away from God. Love, however, makes a sacrifice which satisfies the demands of justice and holiness, enabling us, through faith and repentance, to approach the Almighty and be as familiar with Him as a child with a father. I believe it is time that we Christians, when presenting the gospel, lay the emphasis where God has laid it – on His love.

O God, the greatest thing about You is love. For that I want to say thank You a million times. Amen.

THE ATONEMENT

'OUR GODS DO NOT LOVE US'

Revelation 1:1–8

- -

'To him who loves us and has freed us from our sins ...' (v.5)

A missionary to Greenland preached on God's love. An old chief said, 'Say that again! You mean to tell me your God loves me? Our gods do not love us; they hate us, and they try to kill us. Do you mean to say you have a God who loves?' John Beck talked to him about the love of God until his heart melted, and he became a Christian. A modern-day psychiatrist says, 'The greatest need in man is to be loved.' This is what poor sinners want to bear – and need to hear. Take God's love out of the Christian message, and you take the heart out of it. It's like removing the sun from the heavens.

Father, I see that above all my needs, I need love. And not just any kind of love, but Your love – unconditional love. Amen.

THE GREATEST WORD EVER

John 3:16–21

- - - - - - - - - - - - - - - - - - - -

'For God so loved the world that he gave ...' (v.16)

One preacher searched the Bible for references to God's love but found few in the Old Testament. Many verses presented God as full of wrath, holiness and justice. He then turned to the Gospels and found that the first time in the New Testament where there is a firm and clear declaration that God loves is in John 3:16 – the verse that is before us today. 'It burst upon me,' he said, 'like a ray of sunshine in the darkness. It magnetised my soul as I pondered it.' May it do the same for you as you meditate on it this day.

O Father, help me to put my heart up against Your heart, feel its beat and catch its rhythm. Amen.

THE ATONEMENT

THE CURTAINS ARE OPENED

John 3:16

'For God so loved the world that he gave his one and only Son ...' (v.16)

There can be no possible mistake – God really does love us. This is the first time in the Gospels where the curtains are opened from around the heart of the Deity, and where we see, and see clearly, that the main motivation in the heart of God is unconditional, unquenchable, unsearchable love. But why did it take so long for this fact to be set out in such clear terms? It could not be clearly seen until humanity looked into the face of Jesus. Here humanity is at the end of its long search to find out what God is like. God is love.

O Father, I am so thankful that, at long last, humanity has seen the ultimate truth about You – You are love. Amen.

LOVE DIFFERENTIATES

1 Corinthians 13:1–13

'Love bears all things ...' (v.7, RSV)

God knows how to differentiate between the sin and the sinner. He hates one but loves the other. A pastor tore into a young man who was returning from an evening of drinking and debauchery. When the pastor had finished, the mother got up and without a word walked over and kissed the lips of her son. He broke down and was instantly changed. Afterwards, the man, telling of this turning point in his life, said that he could stand the lashing but he couldn't stand the kiss. Jesus is God's kiss of love placed upon the lips of a reprobate and prodigal humanity.

O God, my Father, You astonish me with Your love. Although I cannot understand it I can enjoy it. Thank You, Father. Amen.

WHAT GOD IS

1 John 4:7–21

'... because God is love ...' (v.8)

One lady said, 'I love Jesus but I don't think very highly of God.' Someone asked her why, and she replied, 'I see God as wanting to send people to hell, and I see Jesus as struggling to stop Him.' Regrettably, this is a view that many have of the atonement. They see the cross as the cause of God's love and not God's love being the reason for the cross. The fact is that Christ did not die *so that* God would love us. Christ died *because* God loved us. The supreme revelation of God is reached in Jesus Christ: God is love.

Father, thank You for showing me that You are not just the author of loving acts, You are love by Your very nature. Amen.

THE BENEFITS OF THE ATONEMENT

FOR READING AND MEDITATION

John 8:31–36

'... *every one who commits sin is a slave to sin.*' (*v.34, RSV*)

Having examined over the past weeks the various aspects of the atonement, we come now to a consideration of its benefits. In what ways does Christ's atoning death benefit us? Firstly, it gives liberty from slavery to sin. Rousseau, in his famous book *The Social Contract*, begins with the blunt assertion that 'Man is born free, yet everywhere he is in chains'. The great mass of mankind, although enjoying physical freedom, is, nevertheless, in moral and spiritual chains. Iron fetters of evil habit hang upon their souls; stout fetters, forged in hell, hold them in the most terrible bondage. They are prisoners to sin. Liberty of soul comes through the Son of God, and the focal point of the power that breaks our moral bondage is found on a hill called Calvary.

Father, when I reflect on the wonder of the fact that I am a ransomed sinner, my gratitude is beyond words. Amen.

THE CHARACTER IT BUILDS

Philippians 3:8–11

*'… not having a righteousness of my own …
but that which is through faith in Christ …' (v.9)*

T he most important thing in life is not building a
career but developing a character. Unfortunately
today's society seems less and less concerned about
character, and more and more concerned about
productivity. Products will pass away but character lives
on from one generation to another. True character can
only be built, however, in co-operation with Christ and
the Holy Spirit by appropriating the righteousness of
Christ. The only thing that will stand the test of time
and eternity is the righteousness of Jesus, which was
manifested on the cross, and which now works in us,
enabling us to do the things that please Him, and making
us truly beautiful in character.

**O Father, help me to be more concerned about my
character than about my career. For Jesus' sake I ask it.
Amen.**

THE PEACE IT PRODUCES

Colossians 1:19–23

'… making peace through his blood,
shed on the cross.' (v.20)

Another way in which Christ's atoning death benefits us is in the peace it produces. War is a gruesome thing. It means the slaughter of the innocent, the destruction of property and the breaking of hearts. The greatest peacemaker the world has seen is our Lord Jesus Christ. The purpose of His coming into the world was to make peace between men and God, and between men and men. The architect of peace is none other than God Himself, for Jesus was God in human form. And why did He compress Himself into a human body? In order to bring peace to a sin-ravaged universe: 'through him to reconcile to himself all things'.

O Lord, I'm so thankful that the peace You died to procure was the peace of victory over sin. Amen.

THE COVENANT IT CONFIRMS

1 Corinthians 11:23–26

'This cup is the new covenant in my blood.'
(v.25, RSV)

Christ's atoning death confirms covenant. In olden days men would cut their arms and hold them together with the other's so their blood would mingle, thus sealing their friendship and ratifying the covenant. Isn't this what Christ has done for us? But His blood, more than mingling with ours, has passed into our spiritual veins. Our blood and humanity have gone into His veins. He has become a partaker of our nature, and we have become partakers of His. We have become one. Our sins go to Him: His righteousness comes to us. The covenant of blood means that we have been fused together as one. Hallelujah!

Jesus, when I see how You have given Yourself to me in blood covenant, I give myself to You – with nothing held back. Amen.

THE DIGNITY IT CONFERS

Revelation 1:4–6

'... and has made us kings and priests ...'
(v.6, NKJV)

The atonement confers dignity. What John is saying, in effect, can be summed up in three terse expressions: He loves us. He frees us. He lifts us. The mitre, as well as the crown, is upon our head. The office to which our Lord calls us is not just regal; it is sacerdotal. In making us priests, God wants us to represent Him to the world and represent the world before Him; to bind it, by the golden chains of prayer, to His feet; to bear its sorrows and carry them in fervent, believing intercession before the throne of grace. We are lifted to the dignity and responsibility of priesthood as well as the splendour of royalty.

Father, thank You for giving me the privilege of not only being a child of God, but of being a priest and a king. Amen.

THE VICTORY IT GAINS

Revelation 12:7–11

*'But they have conquered him by the blood of the
Lamb and by the word of their testimony; they had
to die for it …' (v.11, Moffatt)*

The atonement gains victory. The cross has ended
Satan's power over humanity, and has provided us with
three mighty weapons by which we can overcome him –
the blood of the Lamb, the word of our testimony and the
sacrificial spirit of the cross. Satan's accusations are all met
by the blood of Christ. Martin Luther once picked up a pen
and wrote across the bottom of a list of his sins: 'The blood
of Jesus Christ, God's Son, cleanses from all sin.' Satan has
to withdraw when presented with the claims of Christ's
atoning blood and we have victory over his accusations.

**Thank You, dear Lord, that Your blood is the power by
which I can conquer Satan and his accusations. Amen.**

THE HEAVEN IT PROVIDES

Revelation 21:10–27

'The twelve gates were twelve pearls, each gate made of a single pearl.' (v.21)

The atonement provides a heavenly future. The gates of heaven are pearls. A pearl, it can be said, is really the result of a wound that has been healed as an oyster secretes a precious substance over an invader. That substance becomes a pearl. If there had been no wound, there would have been no pearl. What a picturesque way of saying that the only way into the New Jerusalem is through the innocent sufferings of the Lord Jesus Christ who, on the cross, endured the crushing cruelty of your sin and mine, and turned that pain into a pearl. Our Lord is called by some 'the Pearl of great price'.

Jesus, I'm so thankful that You are the Pearl Gate of great price through which I pass into heaven. Amen.

NOW FOR THE PRACTICE!

Romans 12:1–11

'... I urge you, brothers, in view of God's mercy, to offer your bodies as living sacrifices ...' (v.1)

D oes the truth of the atonement merely lie in our minds as a doctrine or do we invite the Holy Spirit to make it a dynamic force in our lives? Many Christians make the mistake of supposing that when they have listened to a sermon, read a book or followed a series of studies, and given mental assent to what has been said, their religious duty has been discharged, and they may then dismiss the subject from their minds. That is certainly not true of the atonement. For the theory of the cross to be of any value, it must be followed by practice in our lives.

Loving, heavenly Father, help me not to turn back now and enable me to turn theory into practice. In Jesus' name. Amen.

LOOKING OUT – THROUGH A CROSS

FOR READING AND MEDITATION

1 Corinthians 2:1–10

'For I resolved to know nothing while I was with you except Jesus Christ and him crucified.' (v.2)

I looked at the universe through eyes that had never focused on the cross, and what I saw filled me with despair – suffering, pain, sickness, tragedy and death. Then I became a Christian and I learned how to look at life through the cross. I saw a God who entered the struggle, took my sufferings on Himself and became victorious. Now my universe holds steady. The cross saves me from pessimism and despondency. When we learn to look at life through the cross, and realise that the pain, the suffering and the struggles we face can all be transformed to work for higher ends, then, and only then, is the principle of the cross transposed in our lives.

Blessed Lord Jesus, I see clearly now that I can only interpret life in the light of the cross. Amen.

THE ATONEMENT

THE CROSS – INEVITABLE

Luke 14:25–35

'And anyone who does not carry his cross and follow me cannot be my disciple.' (v.27)

Where love and sin meet, a cross arises. It was so in the life of Jesus, and it will be so in your life and mine. The process of growth in Christ will deepen your capacity for suffering. Each new friendship you form, each new injustice you set out to correct, each new sin in others to which you expose yourself, each new enterprise you take on for God, will become a possible suffering point. You must recognise, if you are not to be overwhelmed by life, that a cross becomes inevitable. If you really want to follow your Lord, then you must face the fact that a cross awaits you. It is inevitable.

Lord Jesus, I recognise that the principle of the cross must take place in my life, too. Strengthen me to face its inevitability. Amen.

FOUR MEN WHO BORE CROSSES

1 Peter 2:19–25

'... *Christ suffered for you, leaving you an example, that you should follow in his steps' (v.21)*

It is one thing to see the cross as inevitable; it is another to reach out deliberately and grasp it. On the day of crucifixion, Simon of Cyrene was compelled to carry Christ's cross. The unrepentant thief bore his cross with no repentance or grace. For the penitent thief his cross had meaning – it began in gloom and ended in gladness. The last cross was that of Jesus – a chosen cross. The rest were involuntary – this was voluntary. If a cross is inevitable in life, then don't let it be thrust upon you grudgingly and unwillingly. Anticipate it, accept it and, through it, lift others. Christ's cross was a chosen cross. It is also the Christian's cross.

Father, help me to make the cross I bear redemptive for myself and others. In Jesus' name. Amen.

THE CHRISTIAN'S JOY

Hebrews 12:1–11

'... *who for the joy set before him endured the cross ...*' (v.2)

For some, joy comes when they triumph over others, but it is never lasting. The joy that endures is the joy that comes through doing good to those who spitefully use you – the joy of one who dies for his crucifiers. Anyone who can do that has reached the highest stage of spiritual development, and will experience the kind of joy which throbs in the heart of God. Look out at life, then, not only through the cross, but beyond the cross. There you will see joy – cleansing joy, energising joy, service-inspiring joy. One drop of it puts more oil in the machinery of life than any other known thing.

Father, thank You that the last word about the cross is not pain, but joy. Help me to share it with others. Amen.

A UNIQUE FELLOWSHIP

FOR READING AND MEDITATION

Acts 2:41–47

'They devoted themselves to the apostles' teaching and to the fellowship [koinonia] …' (v.42)

ne of the most important words in the Greek New Testament is *koinonia* (pronounced – coin-own-ia). The coming of the Holy Spirit into the lives of the early Christians produced in their midst a spirit of oneness and unity that excelled anything previously experienced by the people of God in Old Testament times. Nothing quite like it had been seen or known in the annals of history. Such was the high degree of harmony in their relationships, there was no word in their vocabulary to describe it adequately. So they created one – *koinonia*. Unfortunately, in today's Church, the word 'fellowship' doesn't mean quite the same as it did to those early Christians. The word badly needs to be redeemed.

Heavenly Father, help us and restore in our midst the true *koinonia*. In Jesus' name. Amen.

100% FOR CHRIST

1 Corinthians 11:23–32

'But if we judged ourselves, we would not come under judgment.' (v.31)

At an evangelistic meeting where young people were asked to sign a decision form, one girl wrote, 'I am 100% for Christ, but I am only 50% for the Church.' She saw the difference. The Christian Church was not Christian – except in part. She overstated the issue, but there is still enough truth in it to make it sting. Those involved in university and college debates tell us that one thing keeps coming through – people think highly of Christ, but not so highly of the Church. They say, like the girl I have just mentioned, 'We are 100% for Christ but only 50%, or less, for the Church.' It is about time we raised the percentage of Christ in the Church.

O God, give me clear insight and courage to become my greatest critic. For Jesus' sake. Amen.

NOT THE FACTS – BUT THE PERSON

Acts 28:17–31

'... he explained and declared ... and tried to convince them about Jesus ...' (v.23)

An old African chief said, 'We are grateful for the fruits of Christianity – the hospitals, education and so on – but what we need here are the roots – Jesus Christ Himself.' Today, we often speak factually of the cross, the resurrection, the ascension and of Pentecost as though, in themselves, these events were more important than the One with whom they were connected. The Early Church did not preach the crucifixion of Christ; they preached Christ and Him crucified. They did not hold forth on the resurrection of Christ; they preached Christ and the resurrection. Always the main emphasis was on Christ, the Personality. From first to last, Christ must be in the forefront of our service and ministry.

O God, I see so clearly that I must dwell less on the facts and more on Christ's Person. Amen.

MORE OF CHRIST

FOR READING AND MEDITATION

Colossians 3:1–17

----

*'If then you have been raised with Christ ...
aim at and seek the [rich, eternal treasures]
that are above ...' (v.1, Amp)*

Mahatma Gandhi, when asked what he considered
the greatest enemy of Christ in India replied,
'Christianity.' Christianity, the system built up around
Christ, is often the worst enemy of Christ. For instance, a
church noticeboard in one town stated: 'This church is the
only church authorised by God to represent Jesus Christ
in this world.' A woman, believing that her husband, who
belonged to another denomination, would not be raised on
the day of resurrection, stated that she wanted to be buried
in a different part of the cemetery from her husband to
make sure God could tell the difference between them. Is it
any wonder that people say, 'I am 100% for Christ, but only
50% for the Church'?

**O God, forgive us that the system we have built around
You is so contrary to You, and help us change it. Amen.**

HALF CONVERTED

1 Thessalonians 5:14–28

*'And may the God of peace ... separate you
from profane things, make you pure and wholly
consecrated to God ...' (v.23, Amp)*

Many Christians are so taken up with marginal things,
they miss the centre. One writer suggests that the
Magi were converted more to phenomena than they were
to Christ. 'When they saw the star, they rejoiced.' Many
in today's Church are converted more to the phenomena
surrounding Christ than to the Saviour Himself. They are
in the Church all right, but their eyes are focused more
on ritual, ceremony, music or a preacher's eloquence than
they are on the Son of God. There is no daily contact with
the life that flows from Christ, and thus their Christianity
becomes marginal and second-hand. It lacks lustre and
vitality. They are echoes instead of being voices.

**O God, I don't want to be a half converted Christian –
I want to be Yours. 100%. Help me, Lord Jesus. Amen.**

NON-CONFORMIST

Romans 12:1–8

'Do not conform any longer to the pattern of this world, but be transformed by the renewing of your mind.' (v.2)

When we merge with the world, we become submerged. Jesus ate with publicans and sinners, but He never adopted their lifestyle. He was different – that difference made the multitude crowd about Him, to touch Him and be made whole. Although somewhat late, many evangelistic organisations are now beginning to see that to copy the world in order to reach the world is largely non-productive. One evangelistic organisation gave up its emphasis on costume and dress and returned to its emphasis on Christ. Once there, they found they were in their native element. When we are different and do not conform to the world – we are distinctive.

O Father, in an age when conformity seems to be the order of the day, make me a non-conformist. For Jesus' sake. Amen.

'TAKE THESE THINGS HENCE'

Matthew 21:12–16

'"It is written," he said to them, "'My house will be called a house of prayer,' but you are making it a 'den of robbers'."' (v.13)

Christianity, instead of drawing people to Christ, in some cultures, tends to drive people away from Him. If Jesus were here today, He would say to many, as He did to the men who were selling merchandise in the Temple, 'Get these out of here!' (John 2:16). What things? Our petty squabblings, our unnecessary rituals, our misguided ideas, our selfish ways, our silly subterfuges and our foolish bigotries. Christ wants to sweep out of His Church, once and for all, the senseless systems that hide Him from our eyes, and give us a fresh and glorious vision of Himself.

Lord Jesus, speak the word that will bring cleansing and freedom to Your Church. For Your own dear name's sake. Amen.

SHAREHOLDERS IN ETERNITY

FOR READING AND MEDITATION

Jude 1–25

'… I was fully engaged, dear friends, in writing to you about our common salvation …' (v.3, Phillips)

At the heart of the word *koinonia* is the basic word *koinos*, meaning 'common'. *Koinoni*, as we said earlier, means fellowship, but it is a common fellowship, that is, a fellowship in which all are level and all are equal. John Stott says of the word, 'The nouns koinonia (fellowship) and koinonos (a partner) together with the verb koinoneo (to share) all bear witness to what we have in common.' C.H. Dodd, a Greek scholar, writes, 'Koinonoi (plural) are persons who hold property in common, partners or shareholders of a common concern.' As members of the *koinonia*, we are partners with God and with each other, and shareholders in eternity.

Father, thank You for putting me into a fellowship where all are one and where all are equal. Amen.

MORE THAN MATEYNESS

Psalm 133:1–3

'How good and pleasant it is when brothers live together in unity!' (v.1)

When we realise that we share a common inheritance, which is given to us by grace and not through human effort, this produces in us a fellowship which is unique and distinctive. There is nothing quite like it to be found anywhere in society. The genial mateyness of a pub or club is trivial when compared to the potential that exists in the *koinonia*. The stupidities, the inanities, the failures of the Church – I know them all. Nevertheless, there is, flowing through the Church, a common life, a common bond, a common energy, and if we flow with it, it will lift us above all differences and factions to celebrate the true oneness that we have in Christ.

Father, because I am in the Church through You and not through any merit of my own, the more I see the potential for fellowship.

FISHERFOLK

Luke 5:1–11
- - - - - - - - - - - - - - - - - -
'... and so were James, and John ...
Simon's partners.' (v.10)

Christian fellowship is our common share in God's
great salvation. However, fellowship is more than a
sharing in, it involves a sharing out. *Koinonia* concerns not
only what we possess but what we do with what we possess.
Luke uses the word *koinonia* to describe the partnership
relationship of the joint owners of a fishing trade. Paul, in
2 Corinthians 8:23, refers to his co-labourers as his
koinonia, and in Philemon verse 6 speaks of Philemon
sharing out his faith with others (*koinonoi*). As members
of the *koinonia*, we must not just sit back and enjoy its
benefits; we must join hands as partners, like fisherfolk,
in winning men and women to Jesus Christ.

**Father, I see the door of salvation leads me to another
door – the door of service with others. Amen.**

'SAY THIS'

FOR READING AND MEDITATION
Psalm 107:1–9

'Let the redeemed of the LORD say this ...' (v.2)

Most of us came into the Christian life because someone shared their faith with us. And what people did for us – we must do for others. As soon as one finds Christ, there is an impulse to find another and bring them to Christ. This happened with Andrew and Peter. You don't have to be an extrovert type to be a Christian witness. You may be an introvert, and there is nothing wrong with that, providing you are sharing in some way the life that God has given you. Someone has pointed out that of the forty healings recorded in the Gospels, all but seven of the healed were brought to Jesus by someone else.

Father, I see that in the *koinonia* I am a partner in the task of bringing others to know You. Help me. Amen.

A DESIRE FOR EVANGELISM

Psalm 51:1–13

'Restore to me the joy of your salvation …
and sinners will turn back to you.' (vv.12–13)

No one in the *koinonia* is denied spiritual creativity – except those who deny it to themselves. You are made in the inner structure of your being to be expressive. In winning others to Christ we have an opportunity to be creative where it counts. Tilt your will in the direction of evangelism. Most of us have a desire to evangelise, but it never gets further than our mind and emotions. Do not fear failure, for the greatest failure is the failure to do anything. You may feel unworthy because of your past sins, but really you are a tribute of God's grace. Ask God to empower you with the Holy Spirit to reach others.

Father, I bring my life to You for You to fill me with creativity so that I might be an effective Christian witness. Amen.

'AS I HAVE LOVED YOU'

FOR READING AND MEDITATION
John 13:31–35

'... *Love one another. As I have loved you* ...' (v.34)

We are called to love one another, serve one another and support one another in true *koinonia*. When Jesus told us to love one another, He went on to say, 'as I have loved you.' That phrase raised the commandment from the Old (love your neighbour as yourself) to the New – from law to grace. For He loved His disciples, not as they loved each other (or, for that matter, themselves), but with a different type and quality of love – a love that required a special word to express it – *agape*. However, the word 'agape' would be barren had not Jesus filled it with the content of the purest and highest love ever shown on earth.

Father, to discover the meaning of love, real love, all I have to do is look into the face of Jesus. Amen.

LOVED INTO BEING

John 1:35–42

'… *you are … You shall be …*' (v.42, RSV)

Christ loves us, not merely for what we are, but also for what we can be. He said to Simon Peter, 'You are … but you shall be …' It was His love that loved the foreseen Peter into being. We can love the same way. We can love people, not only for what they are, but for what we see they can be. And by our love, we tend to produce the person we see – we love it into being. Love is creative – it finds faith out of the faithless. Above all, spiritual love springs from focusing our eyes on God's love for us, as expressed in the giving of His Son upon the cross.

Father, give me again today a vision of Your love for me, so I begin to love with Your love – the true *agape*. Amen.

THE INVASION OF THE SPIRIT

Acts 2:14–21

---

*'Even on my servants, both men and women,
I will pour out my Spirit ...' (v.18)*

Even after spending three years with Christ, the
disciples appear to finish up in disunity and disarray.
However, when we look at these same disciples in the
Acts of the Apostles, they appear as new and transformed
men. What was it that made the difference? It was the
resurrection of Christ and the coming of the Holy Spirit.
All that Jesus had taught them moved inside them through
the energy and power of the Spirit. Whereas before
truth had been verbal, now it became vital. A divine
reinforcement took place. For three years the disciples had
experienced God with them, now they experienced God in
them. True *koinonia* comes, therefore, by the invasion of
the Holy Spirit.

**O God, I see there can be no true *koinonia* without the
Holy Spirit, so fill my life with Him, I pray. Amen.**

INWARDLY UNIFIED

Acts 4:31–37

- - - - - - - - - - - - - - - - - -

'With great power the apostles continued to testify to the resurrection of the Lord Jesus, and much grace was upon them all.' (v.33)

The coming of the Holy Spirit in the lives of the early disciples meant many things – power, purity, poise and so on – but one of His greatest blessings was the blessing of unity. It was this unity that led to the development of the *koinonia*. The disciples, when they co-operated with God by surrendering their egos to the invading power of the Spirit, found that just as cosmos came out of chaos, when the Spirit moved across the face of the deep and a new universe arose (Gen. 1:3), so the Spirit made a harmonised self arise in each of their lives under a new creative dynamic. They were inwardly unified – hence outwardly unified.

Father, send Your Spirit to make me inwardly whole and unite me with myself so I can be united with others. Amen.

UNITY IN THE IMMEDIATE BODY

FOR READING AND MEDITATION

Acts 2:1–8

'Peter stood up along with the eleven ...'
(v.14, Moffatt)

The Holy Spirit produced unity among the immediate body of believers. At one time Peter stood against the eleven, claiming to be the greatest (Luke 22:7–34) and later he stood among the believers (Acts 1:15). Then the Spirit came and the barriers fell down. The Spirit witnessed that he was to be the spokesman, so he stood up along with the eleven. When he spoke, the eleven spoke in him and through him; it was corporate preaching with corporate results. There was no dispute, no argument as to whom should be spokesman. One with themselves, they were one with each other.

Father, help me not just to be among other believers, but with them for Jesus' sake. Amen.

UNITY AMONGST ALL BELIEVERS

Acts 2:41–47

'The believers all kept together ...' (v.44, Moffatt)

The Early Church was Christ-minded; we are denominationally minded. Paul struck out at the beginnings of denominationalism with these words, 'Is Christ divided?' (1 Cor. 1:13). The idea of dividing into groups around certain teachers with a certain emphasis was abhorrent to the great apostle. His position was this – you don't belong to them, they belong to you. If we destroy the Church by divisions, then God will destroy us by cancelling out our power and influence. The Church today is a fulfilment of this – its influence is destroyed by divisions. The spirit of divisions has replaced the Spirit of God. It's effectiveness is in danger of being destroyed, not from without, but from within.

O Father, let me not unwittingly foster a spirit of division in Your Body. In Jesus' name I pray. Amen.

UNITY IN MATERIAL POSSESSIONS

Acts 2:41–47

'All the believers were together and had everything in common.' (v.44)

T he unity of the Spirit resulted in a unity of possessions. My possessions become our possessions. However, one must bear in mind another verse: 'If a man will not work, he shall not eat' (2 Thess. 3:10). This helps to correct the idea that someone might get what he needs, then refuse to work. If we do not contribute to the collective good, according to our ability, then we should not get according to our need. When the Spirit is at work in the way He manifested Himself in the Early Church, then unity of possessions becomes a direct consequence. But remember that this sharing was not compulsory but voluntary (Acts 5:4).

Father, help me to be a wise and careful custodian of the possessions You have given me – a steward, not a proprietor. Amen.

IS CHRIST A DICTATOR?

FOR READING AND MEDITATION
Luke 6:46–49

- - - - - - - - - - - - - - - - - - -

'Why do you call me, "Lord, Lord," and do not do what I say?' (v.46)

Lenin said, 'Great problems in the lives of people are solved only by force.' Against this monstrous statement, the New Testament stands in complete opposition. Once you introduce force to gain an end, you will have to use force to retain it, and that means dictatorship – the end of free society. The sharing atmosphere in the Early Church was spiritual – it developed out of the Spirit's working in their midst. Some say that the Christian Church is a dictatorship, for Christians submit to Christ's rule in everything. However, it is a dictatorship with a difference. Christ dictates, but His rule rests on laws which He Himself observes, and when we obey His law we find perfect freedom.

O Father, give us intelligent attitudes towards material things, for we cannot impoverish others without getting hurt ourselves. Amen.

UNITY OF RACES

Acts 13:1–12

'Among the prophets and teachers of the church at Antioch were Barnabas and Symeon (also called "The Black Man") …' (v.1, TLB)

The Holy Spirit brings a unity of all races in the Church because all races were equally represented in Christ's death. Simeon the Black, as he was called, possessed an important ministry gift, and exercised it in the church at Antioch. Among others, he laid his hands on Barnabas and Paul to send them forth to preach the gospel to white Europe. By the time the church at Antioch was established, the Early Church had lost its bigotry towards those who were not Jews. The Early Christians, under the Spirit's tutelage, saw through racial prejudice and looked upon every man as a man for whom Christ died.

O God, give me eyes to see everyone as a person for whom Christ died. Remove any prejudices and fears. Amen.

DANGERS TO THE *KOINONIA*

Acts 5:1–11

'Now a man named Ananias ... kept back part of the money for himself ...' (vv.1–2)

What were some of the inner dangers that threatened to destroy the first-century *koinonia*? The first was the issue of money. The fellowship of Christ and His disciples was disturbed when Judas gave way to the love of money, and the fellowship of the Early Church was similarly threatened when Ananias gave way to the same impulse. Someone has said that money and power are the two sources of greatest temptation in the modern Church. How then do we find victory at the place of money? The answer is in self-surrender. Money must be individually surrendered to God so He is our Master and not money or possessions.

Blessed Lord Jesus, help me to renounce money as master, and to realise it as a servant – by Your power. Amen.

IS NEED A GOVERNING PRINCIPLE?

James 2:1–17

'Suppose a brother or sister is without clothes and daily food. If one ... does nothing ... what good is it?' (vv.15–16)

I believe need is a governing principle in relation to the right use of money. Need is basic to life. It is written into our bodies. If we eat less than we need, we become unhealthy; if we eat more than we need, we also become unhealthy. It is also written into our society. If need is an important criteria, then we must ask the Holy Spirit to help us distinguish between a need and a want, for all beyond our actual needs belongs to others. For years I have been guided by this principle. All beyond this belongs to other people, particularly under-privileged Christians.

Father, block me, I pray, when I am about to go beyond my needs, so my money is productive and not paralysing. Amen.

SECRET CRITICISM

Acts 6:1–7

'But with the believers multiplying rapidly, there were rumblings of discontent.' (v.1, TLB)

The word translated here as 'rumblings', is a strong Greek word indicating 'a complaint expressed in subdued tones – secret criticism'. There is nothing wrong with criticism, providing it is presented openly and honestly. What makes criticism dangerous is when it is done covertly, not brought out into the open. If we are to see true *koinonia* in the Christian Church again, then we must make up our minds never to hold secret criticism of one another. We must, of course, welcome constructive criticism, for as someone said, 'The best of us are only Christians in the making.' If we are afraid of criticism then we are living on the defensive; by fear rather than by faith.

Father, help me not to be a secret critic, but give me the courage to share my thoughts in the spirit of Christian love. Amen.

BIGOTRY AND PREJUDICE

Acts 11:1–18

- - - - - - - - - - - - - - - - - -

'But when Peter arrived back ... the Jewish believers argued with him. "You mixed with Gentiles ..." they accused.' (vv.2–3, TLB)

Many Christians 'forbid' others on no more serious ground than that they are not 'one of us' (Mark 9:38–39). Bigotry must not be confused with a determination not to compromise. Firmness of conviction is expected of all Christians. Bigotry arises when, not content with guarding our own convictions, we refuse to look at or listen to the views of others. It is astonishing how much more reasonable the view of another person appears when one listens patiently to it, and tries to understand it. It is right to reason or debate with those who may not see things as we see them. However, when we disagree we must do so without being disagreeable.

Father, deliver me from bigotry and prejudice. Help me show respect to those who differ from me. In Jesus' name. Amen.

A NEW CREATION

Acts 15:13–29

'For it has seemed good to the Holy Spirit and to us to lay upon you no greater burden than these necessary things ...' (v.28, RSV)

egalism was another threat to the *koinonia* of the Early Church. Some teachers in the Church insisted that the Gentiles, in order to be accepted into the Christian family, must submit to the rite of circumcision. What these legalistic teachers failed to see, of course, was the fact that 'in Christ' there is no longer Jew or Gentile, bond or free, but that 'Christ is all, and in all' (Col. 3:11). The Church is not Jewish (though it had Jewish beginnings) and neither is it Gentile. People might be Jews or Gentiles when they come in, but once they are in they leave behind their national or racial identities – they become a new creation.

Father, may I break with all forms of legalism and nationalism, and see myself as first and foremost a citizen of heaven. Amen.

A SPIRIT-LESS GOSPEL

Acts 18:24–19:8

*'... a Jew named Apollos ... a learned man,
with a thorough knowledge of the Scriptures ...
taught about Jesus accurately ...' (vv.24–25)*

A danger threatening the vibrant fellowship was a Spirit-less gospel. Apollos was a good teacher but he knew only 'the baptism of John'. When Paul arrived in Ephesus, he sensed a central lack, so asked what the believers knew of the Holy Spirit. They said, 'we have not even heard that there is a Holy Spirit' (Acts 19:2). There were twelve men in that group, but without the Holy Spirit what did they accomplish? Nothing! The other Twelve (the apostles), filled with the Spirit, were turning the world upside down while the twelve in Ephesus, filled with cultured emptiness, were barely holding their own. No Spirit – no power. It is as simple as that.

**Father, save us from a refined emptiness and give us
the real thing – the power of the Holy Spirit within.
For Jesus' sake. Amen.**

STRONG AND DIFFERING OPINIONS

Acts 15:36–41

'They had such a sharp disagreement that they parted company.' (v.39)

The argument over John Mark got out of hand, and the two apostles decided to part company. J.B. Phillips puts it thus, 'There was a sharp clash of opinion, so much so that they went their separate ways.' Here was a problem that is with us still – strong, spiritual men who differ. How did the Church deal with these strong, spiritual men who differed? As they parted, they were commended by the brothers to the grace of the Lord, as much as to say, 'Brothers, you both need it.' When strong men differ, the Church must always respond this way – by asking God to give them an extra portion of His grace, otherwise *koinoia* might be destroyed.

Father, I pray today for strong leaders in the Church who hold differing opinions. Let Your grace flow. In Jesus' name. Amen.

ALONENESS

Genesis 2:18–25

'It is not good for the man to be alone.' (v.18)

In ordinary life and in the Christian life everyone needs fellowship, and God has provided the means by which we can experience it in a natural family. It is the complex pattern of relationships between parents and children, brothers and sisters which assists our development into adult maturity. The deeper the relationships, the less emotional hang-ups we have when we become adults. It is the lone member of a congregation, who holds himself aloof from Christian fellowship, who is most likely to become spiritually damaged and deprived. Our text lays down more than the principle of marriage. It points to a universal principle – aloneness is not the will of God – fellowship is.

Father, if I am made in my inner being for fellowship, help me establish good relationships with others in Your family. Amen.

UNSHOCKABLE

Romans 12:9–21

- -

'Be devoted to one another in brotherly love.
Honour one another above yourselves.' (v.10)

We are in danger of proximity without community,
closeness without involvement. Deep within the
human heart is an elemental desire for fellowship. Bruce
Larson says of the local pub that 'it is possibly the best
counterfeit there is to the fellowship Christ wants to give
His Church. It is an imitation, dispensing liquor instead
of grace, escape rather than reality, but it is a permissive,
accepting and inclusive fellowship.' God wants His
Church to be a fellowship of people who are unshockable,
sympathetic and accepting – a fellowship where people
can come in and say, 'I'm beat!' 'I'm sinking!' 'I'm
depressed!' without someone hitting them over the head
with a Bible text.

**O God, forgive me for my judgmental attitudes and my
insensitivity. Help me to love and accept others as You
do. Amen.**

SMALL IS BEAUTIFUL

FOR READING AND MEDITATION
Philemon 1–7

'... to the church that meets in your home ...' (v.2)

In order to understand the true nature of the *koinonia*, we must spend some time looking at the function of a small group, for unless we can produce the *koinonia* in a small group, we will never produce it in a large group. Our basic need for fellowship is not completely met by attendance at large meetings of the Church. Crowds have their place, but the *koinonia* must develop first in a small group before it can manifest itself in a large congregation. 'There is always something unnatural and subhuman about large crowds,' says one writer, 'they tend to be aggregations rather than congregations – aggregations of unrelated persons.' We need to relate in small groups, as did the Early Church.

Heavenly Father, help me to be a loving part of a small group to experience the *koinonia*. In Jesus' name. Amen.

A CONSPIRACY OF LOVE

FOR READING AND MEDITATION

Romans 16:1–5

'*Greet also the church that meets at their house.*' (v.5)

A careful examination of the New Testament shows that the house churches usually consisted of small groups of people. For instance, Romans 16:3–5 and Philemon 1–2. They met in large groups from time to time but their spiritual growth and development took place in the small fellowship. Large churches can meet in small groups to foster this *koinonia*. One person says, 'You discover the small group puts a pressure upon you in the right direction. You soon discover you can't let your friends down. Because they expect so much of you, you tend to live up to their expectations.' The *koinonia* is a conspiracy of love, designed to bring out the best in everyone.

O Father, help us to live in fellowship in the conspiracy of love that brings out the best in everyone. Amen.

TRAPPED IN A PEW

Acts 20:13–21

'... I ... have taught you publicly and from house to house.' (v.20)

Dr John Stott, in his book *One People*, says, 'I do not think it an exaggeration to say, therefore, that small groups, Christian family or fellowship groups, are indispensable for our growth into spiritual maturity.' In the small Christian group the participants learn, as George Fox puts it, 'to know each other in that which is eternal.' Elton Trueblood says, 'Once the Church was a brave revolutionary fellowship, changing the course of history; today it is a place where people go to be isolated in a pew or hide behind a pillar. The koinonia turned the world upside down; we go home to turn our dinner plates the right side up.'

Father, help Your Church to produce *koinonia* both in my local community and worldwide. In Jesus' name. Amen.

THE KOINONIA FELLOWSHIP

OPEN HEART SURGERY

James 5:13–20

'Admit your faults to one another and pray for each other so that you may be healed.' (v.16, TLB)

Many small groups fail, although they concentrate on prayer and meditation in the Scriptures, as they give no room for personal sharing. One Church called its small fellowship groups 'The Fellowship of the Open Heart'. Members are encouraged, after a suitable time of prayer and Bible meditation, to share themselves on a deep, personal level. The moment we confess our weaknesses, we merge into a fellowship. However, the moment we tighten up and refuse to acknowledge a fault or weakness, fellowship becomes impossible. It is a sign of immaturity to act as though one has no faults or weaknesses. It is a sign of maturity to confess them and to ask for help in changing them.

Father, help me to acknowledge my need in the presence of my brothers and sisters, wherever and whenever this is possible. Amen.

'WE PLAYED AT HEAVEN'

Hebrews 10:19–25

'And let us consider and give attentive, continuous care to ... studying how we may stir up (stimulate and incite) to love ...' (v.24, Amp)

I once participated in a group where I had the opportunity to share myself as I really was – no masks, subterfuges or unreality. The effect upon my life was astonishing. I would describe it, next to my conversion, as being the most transforming experience of my life. The acceptance I found in the group became a visual aid of how God accepted me, and I discovered subsequently a new understanding and awareness of the Lord. In touching His people, and being touched by them, Christ became more real to me. One person in the group summed it up when she said, 'We played at being in heaven and found we were'.

Holy Spirit, mould us into a living fellowship and give us Your unity in the bond of peace. For Jesus' sake. Amen.

COME TOGETHER

1 Thessalonians 5:1–11

'... encourage one another and build each other up, just as in fact you are doing.' (v.11)

Fellowship is the corporate expression of the Christian life: no corporate life – no effective Christian life. The idea that you can be a solitary Christian, without the corporate relationships provided within the Church, is totally false. There are times when a person, through sickness or for some other reason, is unable to meet with fellow believers, and at such times and under such circumstances, God provides special grace to enable that believer to grow and develop. God's general purpose, however, is that we should come together to encourage and strengthen one another. In the fellowship of the Church, we develop strength and stability that stays with us when confronted by life's trials and adversities.

Father, I thank You for the fellowship of others. May we all encourage and strengthen one another in our faith. Amen.

GOD-GIVEN MINISTRIES

Ephesians 4:1–16

'It was he who gave some to be apostles, some to be prophets, some to be evangelists, and some to be pastors and teachers, to prepare God's people for works of service ...' (vv.11–12)

Sad to say, many local churches are no more than lonely places to which lonely people can go so that all can be lonely together. It is often merely a group of individuals touching elbows on Sunday, and then returning to their isolated individualism. It lacks being a closely-knit fellowship. Unable to find fellowship in the Church, people look elsewhere. However, by the very nature of its constitution and its membership, the Church has the potential to develop into the highest fellowship in the world. One thing is sure – fellowship does not begin with large numbers. It may end there, but it begins with a small, closely-knit group, committed to the principles of New Testament Christianity.

O God, teach us the art of the true *koinonia*, that we might not just be a group of lonely people all lonely together. Amen.

THE KOINONIA FELLOWSHIP

SETTING THE GOAL

1 Peter 1:13–25

'... *see to it that you really do love each other warmly, with all your hearts.*' (v.22, TLB)

A small group is the Church in miniature. When spiritual principles function in a small group in the way they should, then the full fellowship of the Church functions the way it should. The goal of small groups should be to develop the three aspects of the *koinonia*: sharing in, sharing out and sharing with. Sharing in means discussing the faith so that, through prayer and discussion, we come to a greater awareness of God. Sharing out means considering what service God wants your group to give to the community. Sharing with means learning to care for one another in love, bearing one another's burdens and making Jesus' love a reality.

Father, guide me so that I might come to learn and express the true meaning of the *koinonia*. In Jesus' name. Amen.

AROUND THE WORD

Psalm 119:9–16

'I meditate on your precepts and consider your ways.' (v.15)

A fellowship group ought to be engaged in devotional Bible study and prayer. I say devotional Bible study because the Christian life rises and falls at the point of the devotional. In devotional Bible study one sets out not so much to instruct the mind, but to inflame the heart. The whole object is to feed on Christ through His Word. It is important that a passage be understood in its context, but one must go beyond that to discover its up-to-date message. That message must then be allowed to speak to the heart, to the mind and to the conscience. Everything should be done in a relaxed manner avoiding, as you would a plague, the classroom atmosphere.

Father, help us to use Your Word, not merely to instruct our minds, but to fire our spirits. Amen.

GOD'S PART – OUR PART

Ephesians 4:1–7

'Make every effort to keep the unity of the Spirit through the bond of peace.' (v.3)

The unity of the Spirit (fellowship) is created for us by God, but we must work at maintaining it. The small group, when run on proper lines, accomplishes that. Sometimes the group will engage in prayer or praise. The presence of the Spirit in the group will give point and direction to the prayer life of the group. The group could also break bread together. Christ always makes Himself known in the 'breaking of bread'. Formality should be at a minimum. Don't give way to the temptation, however, to have no form or structure. The group life must be organised around embodied objectives and not around hazy ideas if it is to function effectively.

O God, help me, when I am in a group, to be the kind of person I want others to be. Amen.

STRAIGHTEN YOURSELVES OUT

2 Corinthians 13:8–14

'Finally, then, my brothers ... agree with one another and live out peace.' (v.11, Phillips)

An individual, in order to be healthy, must be outgoing. The same applies to a group. Without some outward common concern and service, the fellowship of the group will become maimed. The last aspect of *koinonia* is 'sharing with'. If anyone is hurting they should be encouraged to share their hurt. People come into a group with many barriers: fears, anxieties, resentments, inhibitions, guilt and so on. Public sharing of faults and weaknesses is a great healer, particularly when accompanied by prayer. This does not mean that everything has to be shared, but only as much as we think God wants us to share.

O God, help us to bring up things that fester in our souls. And then we shall be healed. Amen.

'ALL CLAMMED-UP'

Ephesians 4:25–32

- -

'Finish, then, with lying … for we are all parts of the same body.' (v.25, Phillips)

Many people are clammed up and afraid to share their feelings. When you want to encourage someone else to open up to you, open up to them. In one group, I shared some of my own anxieties, fears and inhibitions. It was like pulling a log out of a log jam! The result was that the group came to a new level of awareness both of themselves and of each other and of God. When we open up to each other, we find that we carry that same openness into our relationship with God. And the more open we are to Him, the more of Himself He can pour into us.

Father, thank You for showing me that in bringing things to the surface, I am not shaming myself but saving myself. Amen.

LIFE IS CORPORATE

1 Corinthians 12:12–26

'For the body does not consist of one member but of many.' (v.14, RSV)

What are some of the principles we should embody if we are to live together well with others? Firstly, we should recognise that life is corporate. Many look upon life as an individual thing, and in consequence they are continually in trouble with other people. A cancer cell, I am told, is one that ceases to minister to the rest of the body and insists on being ministered to – it is, therefore, cancerous instead of contributive. There are many Christians who are cancerous in today's Church; they look at what they can get from the whole, instead of what they can give to the whole. They are getters – not givers.

Lord Jesus, teach me how to live well with others for I know that I want others to live well with me. Amen.

MISSING FROM THE MEETING

John 20:24–29

'... *Thomas ... one of the twelve, was not with the disciples when Jesus came.' (v.24)*

Make it your goal to get together in fellowship as often as you can. Thomas missed one of the meeting times of the apostles, and thus missed what could have been one of the greatest moments of his life. Later, however, he met with the group, and what was the result? He met the Lord. When we meet with others, we meet with Jesus. Be loyal to the group. This means that you will never criticise any member behind their back. There can be no real fellowship if secret criticism takes place. Once everyone knows that there is no secret criticism, then this produces confidence. And confidence produces freedom.

O God, in this difficult, delicate but delightful business of getting on with others, give me the skill and patience I need. Amen.

BEING WITH THE GROUP

Malachi 3:16–18

'Then those who feared the LORD talked with each other, and the LORD listened and heard.' (v.16)

Decide to be one with the group, not just a part of it. Just to sit with a group doesn't necessarily imply fellowship. There must be something more than being in the group, you must be with the group. So the first thing to do in a group, like an orchestra, is to tune up all the instruments to one another and to God. Don't try to dominate the group. This is fatal, for it encourages the same thing in others, and then the stage is set for clash and strife. Instead of domination, try co-operation. At the threshold of all successful corporate living is self-surrender.

Father, drive deep into my spirit the truth that You have put me in a fellowship, not to dominate it, but to develop it. Amen.

BE BIG

Philippians 4:1–9

*'Let all men know and perceive and recognise
your unselfishness – your considerateness, your
forbearing spirit.' (v.5, Amp)*

Be willing to give way in small things that don't involve
important principles. 'The bigness of a person,' says
a famous philosopher, 'can be judged by the size of the
things upon which he takes his stand.' One of the great
lessons of life is to keep small things small and big things
big. We often reverse these things in our relationships
with one another. Be prepared, when necessary, to side
with the group against yourself. Sometimes God shows
us something about ourselves through a group that we
cannot see when we are alone. We must be sensitive to
the opinions of others in our group, for they might see
something we cannot.

**Father, teach me to be an effective and contributing
member of Your Church. For Jesus' sake. Amen.**

WHO IS PERFECT?

James 3:1–13

'We all stumble in many ways. If anyone is never at fault in what he says, he is a perfect man, able to keep his whole body in check.' (v.2)

Accept people as they are. We must accept ourselves, and others, as we are if we are to enjoy good relationships in the Christian community. If we expect others to be perfect, we are bound for disappointment and disillusionment. Jesus chose the Twelve, not because He found them to be perfect, but because He knew they longed to be different. Remember, you have to get along with yourself despite yourself, so make up your mind to get along with others in spite of themselves. Don't use the group for your own purposes. It can be sensed at once if you are trying to use the group for ulterior motives. Remember, be a giver, not a getter.

Father, make me a giver not just that I might get, but that I might be what You want me to be. Amen.

THE KOINONIA FELLOWSHIP

WALKING IN THE LIGHT

1 John 1:1–9

'But if we walk in the light, as he is in the light, we have fellowship with one another ...' (v.7)

Another principle of group growth is to be ready and willing to confess faults. Whenever we begin to confess our faults, we merge into a fellowship. But the moment we tighten up and refuse to acknowledge our faults, fellowship becomes impossible. Meet any negative issues which arise before they get cold. If you harbour a thing in your heart, it will fester. Jesus said, 'Settle matters quickly with your adversary ...' (Matt. 5:25). When Jesus met any issue, He never hesitated to deal with it right there and then, and if you are to know peace in your relationships, so must you.

Lord Jesus, I am so thankful that You did not hesitate in meeting issues. Give me that same nerve I pray. Amen.

'MEMBERS ONE OF ANOTHER'

FOR READING AND MEDITATION

Romans 12:1–8

'... so in Christ we who are many form one body, and each member belongs to all the others.' (v.5)

Keep in mind that we are different members of one Body. This thought alone ought to protect us from all kinds of jealousy. If we are members one with another, then someone else in the group makes up for any deficiency we may have, and complements where we are weak. None of us has everything. However, we all have something. This attitude will help fill us, not with jealousy, but with pride – pride that as members together in the Body of Christ, we can be so effective and efficient. The whole point is that, in a group, the strength of any is the strength of all.

Father, help me to bring to all my relationships Your unfailing patience and love. In Jesus' name I pray. Amen.

THE KOINONIA FELLOWSHIP

WHEN FELLOWSHIP BREAKS DOWN

Colossians 3:1–14

'Bear with each other and forgive whatever grievances you may have against one another.' (v.13)

What do we do when fellowship is broken by a serious disagreement? As believers we are under an obligation to try and restore a relationship; not to attempt to do so is to deny the reality of the *koinonia*. It is impossible to live on close terms with Jesus Christ if we are not in a right relationship with the rest of His family, be it a member of our group or anyone else in the wider Body of Christ. If I refuse to forgive someone then, however much I compensate for it by Christian activity, I will experience an inner bondage that will cripple my spiritual effectiveness.

Lord Jesus, do not withhold Your scalpel if You see I need a spiritual operation. For Your own dear name's sake. Amen.

GOD'S GUIDELINES

FOR READING AND MEDITATION
Matthew 18:15–20

'If your brother sins against you, go and show him his fault … If he listens to you, you have won your brother over.' (v.15)

The responsibility to take action over a broken relationship always lies with you. This is true not only if a brother sins against you, but when you sin against your brother. Going to someone whom you have hurt, or who has hurt you, has been and always will be the greatest test of genuine love. First, however, before going to someone who has hurt you, you should examine yourself to see if you have failed in a similar area in your own life. The things we dislike in others are often unconscious weaknesses in our own lives. We need to take the beam out of our own eye before taking the splinter out of another's.

Father, help me not to be a mere hearer of Your Word, but a doer, in order to fully restore broken relationships. Amen.

CONFRONT BUT DON'T CONDEMN

Galatians 6:1–10

'… if someone is caught in sin, you who are spiritual should restore him gently.' (v.1)

When you are sure that there is nothing you need to put right, then you must confront the person who has hurt you. But the confrontation must always be without condemnation. The purpose of confrontation is that of restoration. If you go to a person simply to expose him, to show him up and tell him what a fool he has been, then you are not going to him in the spirit of today's text. You are taking the position of a judge, and that, according to Scripture, is wrong. The more you humble yourself, the more God is able to minister grace through you to others.

O Father, teach me how to confront without condemning, to restore without exposing. For Jesus' sake. Amen.

MEET IN PRIVATE

FOR READING AND MEDITATION
Proverbs 25:1–12

'So discuss the matter with him privately.'
(v.9, TLB)

I f you tell anyone else about an offence a brother has committed before telling him, you create several problems. Firstly, you demonstrate that you don't really love the brother concerned, or even the Lord, for if you did you would follow your Master's prescription for dealing with broken relationships. Secondly, you might encourage the person you are sharing with to adopt an attitude of enmity to the offender. Thirdly, you damage the effectiveness of your approach to the offender because it is not based on the principles set out in Scripture. The motivation for dealing with issues is to win a brother rather than to condemn him. If that motive is not there, relationships will not rightly be restored.

Father, help me to submit to Your Word in everything – even when it cuts right across my own inclinations. Amen.

JUDGMENT AND DISCERNMENT

Matthew 7:1–12

'Do not judge, or you too will be judged.' (v.1)

Judging another is sin, but discerning another's spiritual condition is something we might need to do as 'witnesses'. How do we know when we are discerning and not judging? We discern another person's problem when we make sure that we have taken the beam out of our own eye, when we are motivated by a desire to restore and not to expose, when we ask questions until all relevant factors are understood, when we seek to discover the root cause and not just focus on the symptoms and when we approach a person who is in need of correction in a spirit of Christlike love. Such people would be witnesses for someone before they are witnesses against someone.

Father, help me to be a person who does not judge others but, with the help of Your Spirit, uses discernment to help others. Amen.

A CLEANSED CHURCH

Acts 5:1–11

- - - - - - - - - - - - - - - - -

'With his wife's full knowledge he kept back part of the money for himself …' (v.2)

I t is important that other 'witnesses' and the Church see their role in conflict not as judges, but as restorers. If this is done in the right spirit then the Church will see it as a cleansing agent in their midst – evidence that unbiblical behaviour must be dealt with, for it is usually true that when one member stumbles, there are many others with the same, if not a similar, weakness. A church's position should be one of dependency on the Holy Spirit. Prayer, fasting and self-examination should be entered into, and when the offender sees the humbling effect on the church, they may be motivated toward repentance.

Father, make me a pure member of my own community, and Your Church a place of purity and power. Amen.

A CLEANSED COMMUNITY

1 Peter 4:12–19

'For it is time for judgment to begin with the family of God ...' (v.17)

If a person fails to heed the correction of the church then Matthew 18:15–18 says: 'treat him as you would a pagan.' This doesn't mean that the person should be ignored and not spoken to, but that members of the fellowship refrain from entering into the same kind of close relationship with them as they have with each other. When a person is de-fellowshipped, the church should commit the person to God in prayer, and pray that, through the action taken, God will be glorified. If, at some time, the person repents and deals with the basic problem, then they should be accepted into the fellowship with as much rejoicing as a sinner who comes in for the first time.

Father, forgive us for failing to apply the truth of Your Word to the daily life of Your Church. In Jesus' name. Amen.

GIVING A GOOD REPORT

FOR READING AND MEDITATION
Proverbs 15:20–33

*'Pleasant sights and good reports give happiness
and health.' (v.30, TLB)*

I n some churches, each member of a fellowship makes
a commitment to give only a good report of others,
and never to give a bad report unless they have first been
to the person concerned and followed the principles of
Matthew 18. The value of such a commitment is that it
eliminates all forms of gossip, backbiting and disharmony
in a fellowship, for when strife and unrest is allowed to
continue in the midst of God's people, there can be no true
koinonia. As one member of a fellowship said, when this
policy was introduced: 'It gives me a marvellous feeling to
know that no one would give a bad report about me before
checking with me first.'

**Father, help me to face this challenge now, and come
out on the side of love, for I can never be too loving.
Amen.**

ASSUME RESPONSIBILITY

Matthew 12:22–37

'... *men will have to give account on the day of judgment for every careless word they have spoken.*' (v.36)

What is a bad report? It is using words that put someone else in a bad light. It is damaging someone else's reputation with information that does not need sharing. It is encouraging or spreading discontent, gossip or discord amongst others. It is possible, of course, to give a bad report of someone without using words – by gestures, facial expression or tone of voice. Actually we can say more through negative facial expressions and gestures than we can through our words. What a revolution would take place in our churches and fellowships if we all committed ourselves to giving only good reports. I am convinced that such a practice can bring about a transformation in our interpersonal relationships.

Father, may my words, gestures and tone of voice all combine to speak Your message of love and truth. Amen.

RIGHT PRINCIPLES

James 1:19–27

'If anyone considers himself religious and yet does not keep a tight rein on his tongue, he deceives himself ...' (v.26)

How do you stop someone giving a bad report about someone else to you? As soon as you realise that someone is giving you a bad report about another person, stop them and say: 'Are you telling me this so that I might be a witness in restoring this person according to Matthew 18?' If they are not, then lovingly suggest that as you are not directly involved (if this should be the case) then you would prefer not to hear it. If someone persists then walk away. Keep before you the principle that, as a Christian, your main motivation is always to restore in openness and love and not to revile in secret criticism.

Lord, give me the grace and wisdom I need to follow through on Your principles so You can be glorified in all my relationships. Amen.

THE KOINONIA FELLOWSHIP

A DAY OF DECISION

Proverbs 6:16–19

'There are six things which the LORD hates ...
which are an abomination to him ... a man who
sows discord among brothers.' (vv.16,19, RSV)

Consider making the following commitment:

In obedience to the Word of God, I hereby commit myself
to the goal of giving a good report. When this is not
possible I shall remain silent or go privately to the person
concerned and explain the offence or problem preventing
me from giving a good report of them. I propose to
approach an offender in a spirit of genuine love, having first
examined and corrected my own attitudes and actions. Only
if I am unable to restore an offender will I share the problem
with others, according to the principles of Scripture. When
I violate this goal I shall ask forgiveness, knowing that God
resists the proud but gives grace to the humble.

**Father, help me at this moment, for I truly want to be
a member of Your Body of whom You can be proud.
Amen.**

DO IT AGAIN, LORD!

James 4:1–10

'... *The Spirit Whom He has caused to dwell in us yearns over us and He yearns for the Spirit (to be welcome) with a jealous love ...' (v.5, Amp)*

The *koinonia* of the Early Church can happen again, wherever the hearts of God's people meet His conditions. The same Holy Spirit who came at Pentecost and made the Early Church into what Elton Trueblood called an 'incendiary fellowship', is with us still. God is yearning jealously over His Church at this present time, eager to dwell in the midst of it, eager to see it experience the true *koinonia*. It is the destiny of every Christian to be a part of the *koinonia* – the only thing that can block it is our stubbornness and wilfulness. One thing is sure, the Church is mature as an institution to the degree that it can, and does, produce the *koinonia*.

Father, I dedicate myself afresh to the prayerful task of bringing in the *koinonia*. For Your praise, Your honour and Your glory. Amen.

THE KOINONIA FELLOWSHIP

JULY 1
CREATED TO PRAISE

FOR READING AND MEDITATION

Psalm 9:1–20

'I will praise You, O LORD, with my whole heart; I will tell of all Your marvellous works.' (v.1, NKJV)

Thanking God and praising God are quite distinct and separate – we praise God for who He is, we thank Him for what He does. We must not hold to these distinctions too rigidly, as sometimes they merge into each other. Why were we created? The best answer to that question is contained in the words of *The Westminster Catechism*: 'Man's chief end is to glorify God and enjoy Him forever.' In other words, we were created to praise. Learn to praise the Lord at all times – up times, down times, dark times, bright times – and I promise you that life will soon take on a new and different meaning.

God, forgive me for the times I take blessings for granted, rather than receiving them with gratitude. May I praise You at all times. Amen.

AT ALL TIMES?

Psalm 34:1–22

'I will extol the LORD at all times; his praise will always be on my lips.' (v.1)

The psalmist tells us that he praised God 'at all times'. Can we really be expected to praise God on all occasions and at every opportunity? Surely it means most, or many or almost all times. One can't be expected to be full of praise when the days are dark and grey, or the doctor is calling every day, looking graver each time he leaves. Not so: 'I will bless the LORD at all times,' says the psalmist, 'his praise will always be on my lips.' Take a leaf out of the psalmist's book and follow his advice – make this day a day of continued praise.

O Father, this day I want to be filled with unceasing praise. For Jesus' sake I ask it. Amen.

HYMN NINETY-TWO

FOR READING AND MEDITATION
Psalm 33:1–22

'*Sing joyfully to the LORD ...*' (v.1)

A minister went to preach in an unfamiliar church and was told just before the service that every Sunday the front pews were occupied by the residents of a local home for the blind. He wondered if that day they might like to select one of the hymns. They wanted hymn number ninety-two. Ninety-two? He knew it well: 'When all Thy mercies, O my God, My rising soul surveys, Transported with the view, I'm lost in wonder, love, and praise.' Though physically blind, this is what they wanted to sing. Will we, who can see, refuse to open our eyes and magnify Him for His mercy?

Father, there are a thousand things for which I ought to be grateful. Help me to be so. For Jesus' sake. Amen.

FIXED!

Psalm 108:1–13

'O God, my heart is fixed; I will sing and give praise ...' (v.1, AV)

Fixed! What an exciting word to begin a day with. A life that is firmly fixed in God and established on the Saviour's love must inevitably know a deep assurance and an abiding joy. In such a situation, praise flows as naturally as water from a spring. We must dwell on this fact until it begins to turn over the machinery of our soul – that in Christ our hearts are fixed, held solid by the firm hands of a loving God. Nothing can move you from your anchorage in God. Show me a man or woman who aligns themselves with this truth and I will show you a person who is full of praise.

O God, as I focus on the fact that my life is firmly fixed in You, I become full of praise. Amen.

EXUBERANT PRAISE

Isaiah 43:1–21

'... the people I formed for myself that they may proclaim my praise.' (v.21)

I can never understand how it is that over the centuries the Christian religion has become associated with gloom. Even in Old Testament times, praise was vocal and vociferous. The Early Church was so joyful on the Day of Pentecost that they were accused of being drunk. Modern Christians do not come under this dark suspicion! The first Franciscans had to be reproved for laughing in church because they were so radiantly happy. The early Methodists took some of their tunes from operas and set their songs to dance music. General Booth told the first Salvationists that if they felt the Spirit moving them during a hymn or prayer, they could jump. They did!

O God, make us once again a people of praise. Help us to be exuberant, joyful and infectiously happy. For Jesus' sake. Amen.

WHAT'S HAPPENED TO US?

Psalm 100:1–5

'Enter his gates with thanksgiving and his courts with praise ...' (v.4)

Saints of previous generations manifested a joy and an exuberance that in some sections of today's Church would be greatly frowned upon. What has happened to us? Dr Sangster wrote, 'It is when the fires in the individual heart die down that convention frowns on exuberance and an air of superiority is affected toward those who cannot restrain their joyous praise.' Church history is full of instances showing that when a movement of the Spirit begins, those involved in it demonstrate an unrestrained delight that later gives way to formalism and convention. Do not be discouraged by those like David's wife Michal (2 Sam. 6:16) who will abhor any semblance of joy, and will murmur something about fanaticism and emotionalism.

O God, forgive us for being so sober and dignified that it appears we have no joy and nothing to celebrate. Amen.

SELAH!

Psalm 84:1–12

'… they are ever praising you. Selah.' (v.4)

A word occurs often in the book of Psalms – *selah*! The translators, instead of giving the Hebrew word an English interpretation, simply let it remain. Commentators are divided on its usage but a good argument can be made for the fact that amongst other things it appears in the Psalms to indicate a musical climax or a burst of praise. The Psalms were not said, but sung, and there were times when the singers were bidden to become more exultant in their worship and to swell their voices in more enthusiastic praise. To mark such moments, the word *'selah'* was introduced. May our hearts, too, burst with praise.

Father, teach me to enter into the praise that never ceases while I am here on earth. For Jesus' sake. Amen.

DOES GOD NEED OUR PRAISE?

Ephesians 5:5–21

'... *always giving thanks to God ...*
for everything ...' (v.20)

hy does God insist on being praised? When I first
became a Christian, the idea that God craved praise,
like a vain woman angling for compliments, was abhorrent
to me. Then someone gave me a book in which the author
pointed out that while God does not need our praise ('it is
not in our power to add to His plenitude'), He delights in it
nevertheless. The author told the story of a Sunday school
teacher who received a cheap penknife as a present from
one of his little scholars. It was the product of hoarded
halfpennies. Did he need it? No! Did he want it? Yes!

**Father, I see that I can bring joy and delight to Your
heart through my praise. So I give it freely, joyously
and perpetually. Amen.**

PRAISE DOES US GOOD

James 5:10–20

'... *those who have reason to be thankful should*
continually be singing praises to the Lord.'
(v.13, TLB)

I f God doesn't need our thanks, then why does He so
often encourage us, through His Word, to be thankful?
The answer is simple, though it must not be considered
simplistic: we need it. It does us good to be thankful. In
one sense, being thankful does more for us than it does
for God. Modern-day psychology has discovered that we
are not made happy by what we acquire but by what we
appreciate. In other words, the degree to which we are
thankful or appreciative determines our happiness in every
area of life. That is why six-month-old acquisitions often
give us much less happiness than when they were new.

O God, teach me the art of continual thankfulness
and to appreciate all Your blessings to me. Help me,
Lord Jesus. Amen.

A WRONG FOCUS

1 Thessalonians 5:14–23

'*... give thanks in all circumstances, for this is God's will for you ...*' (v.18)

Many of us live on the borders of neuroticism because we fail to recognise the blessings of God in our lives. Someone once wrote to me, 'For weeks I had been going about concentrating on the difficulties in my life, and had become deeply depressed. Then something you said in *Every Day with Jesus* caused me to look at the good things that were happening to me, and instantly the depression lifted.' This letter does not surprise me for I have come to see that life works in one way – if we focus on our difficulties, we will get depressed; if we focus on God's mercies, we will be uplifted.

Father, teach me that I am fulfilled not by what I possess but by what I am thankful for. For Jesus' sake. Amen.

THE PURPOSE AND POWER OF PRAISE

BETTER FOR THE PRAISING

Psalm 150:1-6

- - - - - - - - - - - - - - - - - - -

'Let everything alive give praises to the Lord!
You praise him! Hallelujah!' (v.6, TLB)

God is the only Being in the universe who needs no one else to complete Him. We, on the other hand, are completed by praise, and when we fail to give or show appreciation we experience impoverishment. Imagine standing before Niagara Falls and feeling nothing. You would be the loser! To admire, appreciate and praise God is to be awake, alert and aware of reality. Not to admire Him or praise Him is to lose out on life, for this is what we were originally designed for. We praise Him and bring delight to His heart, but, at the same time, we are made better by the praising.

Father, just as blood in my body carries sustenance and flushes out impurities, so let praise sustain and purify me. In Jesus' name. Amen.

EXPRESSION DEEPENS IMPRESSION

Psalm 107:1–43

- -

'Has the Lord redeemed you? Then speak out!
Tell others he has saved you ...' (v.2, TLB)

I t is a law of life that expression deepens impression. Have you ever found yourself sharing with someone about a pleasant experience you had, only to find that as you share it you feel a warm inner glow that surpasses even the joy you knew in the experience itself? That was the law of 'expression/impression' at work. Dr Sangster said, 'One of the worst moments for an atheist is when he feels thankful and has no One to thank.' How sad to watch a glorious sunset and not be able to thank the One who designed it. How sad to look at God's glory and love and not thank Him or tell others.

My God and Father, the more praise I express, the more I have to express. And the cycle will never end. Amen.

'AND THAT IS HEAVEN'

Revelation 4:1–11

'Day and night they never stop saying:
"Holy, holy, holy is the Lord ..."' (v.8)

I once thought of heaven, I am afraid, as a kind of interminable church service. Imagine being in a state where you are in perfect love with God, satiated with Him, drunk with Him, overwhelmed by a delight which, far from being pent-up within you, flows out in free and unrestrained expression. Imagine, too, what it would be like to express the praise you feel freely, without restriction or inhibition. In the giving and expressing of such praise, a human being would experience such delight and overwhelming joy, which would fill his personality to its utmost limits. And that is heaven!

O Father, I can't wait to meet You and to praise You with unrestricted joy. Amen.

NOT A DEMAND – AN OFFER

Matthew 16:21–28

'… whoever loses his life for me will find it.' (v.25)

Through the process of praise God is able to communicate His presence more fully to us. As we give ourselves to Him in praise, He, in turn, is able to give Himself to us. Why should this be? It is as if God is saying, 'Nothing of value can be received in this universe without self-giving. As you go through the door of self-giving, and focus upon Me in adoration and praise, so I am able to move through that same door and validate My presence in your hearts.' Seen in this light, His insistence on being praised is not so much a demand but an offer.

Father, when You insist on my praise it is my interests You have at heart – not Your own. I am eternally grateful. Amen.

THE ROOT OF SIN

Daniel 5:13–31

'…. the God in whose hand is your breath, and whose are all your ways, you have not honoured.'
(v.23, RSV)

Eve made a free decision to focus on the thing she was denied rather than thank God for the many other things He had provided. A neurotic is usually obsessed by what he lacks, instead of being thankful for what he has. God reprimands Belshazzar for failing to recognise that He was the source of his existence. The apostle Paul told the Christians in Rome a similar truth when he said, '… men are without excuse. For although they knew God, they neither glorified him as God nor give thanks to him …' (Rom.1:20–21). Thanklessness lies at the root of mankind's sin and most of our everyday sins as well!

O God, save me I pray from the sin of thanklessness and help me to be continually thankful. For Jesus' sake. Amen.

PRAISE IS GOOD FOR US

Psalm 92:1–15

'It is good to give thanks to the LORD, to sing praises to thy name ...' (v.1, RSV)

Praising God and others is good for us. A doctor once told me that the happiest and healthiest people are those who are quick to praise – not the flatterers or the insincere, but those who look for and who are quick to recognise the praiseworthy aspects of every situation. Dyspeptics, I am told by those who work in the medical profession, are notorious grumblers. Is their dyspepsia due to their inner disharmony? Perhaps. One thing is sure, when we fail to praise that which is good and worthy of recognition, we are depleted, starved, poisoned and lose our sense of wellbeing.

Father, help me to be a happy, healthy person who can quickly recognise praiseworthy aspects of every situation. Amen.

THE PURPOSE AND POWER OF PRAISE

INNER DIVISION

Colossians 3:1–15

'Let the peace of Christ rule in your hearts,
since … you were called to peace.' (v.15)

Someone has defined praise as 'inner health made audible'. What is the connection between a readiness to praise and inner and outer health? We are made in our inmost beings for praise. God designed us to be praising beings, and if this is not our chief characteristic, the machinery of life gets out of gear – for we are geared to creation. Our first responsibility, of course, is to praise God, but we have a responsibility, too, to praise others. Some are vociferous in their praise of God but extremely grudging in their praise of others. Such a person will never be truly happy (or healthy) because he is a divided being.

Father, help me to be a whole person – not a divided one. I want to be at one with You and others. Amen.

'MADE FOR HIM'

Colossians 1:9–20

'... all things were created by him,
and for him.' (v.16)

God's laws are written not only in the Bible, they are written into our very beings. We were 'Made by Him and for Him'. We were created to praise. 'After I have spent some time praising the Lord,' said a Christian surgeon 'my blood flows better in my veins.' 'My glands function better when I am tuned in to the Almighty,' said another medical man. As the stomach and food, the seed and the soil are made for each other, so is our being made for praise. Praise is good for you – good for your mind, your body, your spirit and your relationships. Being niggardly with your praise is bad for you – bad for your mind, body, spirit and relationships.

Father, You designed me to be a praising person.
Help me to make this the chief characteristic of my life.
Amen.

LOADED WITH BENEFITS

Psalm 68:1–19

'Blessed be the Lord, who daily loads us with benefits ...' (v.19, NKJV)

Praise is the right thing to do because to take benefits from God without a thought or a word of thanks is mean and contemptible. Even a dog wags its tail when given a bone. Being thankful for the good things that come to us rather than just grumbling about the bad things that go on around us, helps us to keep our minds balanced and functioning in the way God designed them to. If we are alert we can see something to be grateful for in even the most dark and dismal circumstances. To see His love, you have only to look.

Father, give me eyes to see Your goodness, and when I see it, help me not merely to look at it, but give thanks. Amen.

THE LEAP OF FAITH

FOR READING AND MEDITATION
Mark 11:20–26

'Have faith in God ...' (v.22)

I once read of a little girl who detested milk pudding, but was made to eat some for dinner. When she asked if she might get down from the table, her mother said, 'Yes, when you have returned thanks.' 'But I have nothing to be thankful for,' she said sulkily. 'Very well,' said her mother, 'then stay there until you have.' There was silence for several minutes, and then she piped up rather jauntily, 'Thank God I wasn't sick. Now may I get down?' We must not falsely invent reasons for praise. We can take the leap of faith and believe that somewhere at the heart of any problem God is working for good.

Father, thank You that You are with me in every situation and so there is always something to praise You for. Amen.

THE SACRIFICE OF PRAISE

FOR READING AND MEDITATION

Hebrews 13:5–21

'… let us continually offer to God a sacrifice of praise …' (v.15)

When cancer strikes, it isn't easy to be a praising person, though I am surprised at the number of times, when talking to Christians who have succumbed to this dreadful disease, so many of them find reasons to be grateful. The ministry of praise at such times may be what the Bible terms 'the sacrifice of praise' – thanksgiving that has blood upon it. There are Christians who are so in touch with God that they believe God's love surrounds them even when they are overtaken by a tragedy. It strains faith and taxes it to its utmost limit, but saints down the ages rise up to testify that it is possible. The *sacrifice* of such thanksgiving is, indeed, precious in God's sight.

O God, give me the kind of faith that trusts You even when it can't trace You. For Jesus' sake. Amen.

VICTORY THROUGH PRAISE

2 Chronicles 20:1–24

'As they began to sing and praise, the LORD set ambushes against the men ... and they were defeated.' (v.22)

Praise often plays a prominent part in turning defeat into victory. Jehoshaphat laid out his problem before the Lord in fear and trembling. In the midst of his intercession, God showed him the secret of victory. He was to place in the forefront of his army a selected group of singers whose task it was to go ahead of the army, singing and praising the Lord. It sounds like a pretty far-fetched idea, doesn't it? The secret of this story is found in verse 15: '... the battle is not yours, but God's.' We may not understand how praise brings victory, but then we are not called to understand – we are called to stand.

Lord, help me to see that praise is a proven path to victory, and enable me to practise it – today. Amen.

THE FALL OF JERICHO

Joshua 6:1–20

*'… make all the people give a loud shout;
then the wall of the city will collapse …' (v.5)*

We don't know what the Israelites shouted, but I feel quite sure myself it was a shout of praise. The example of Joshua and the destruction of the walls of Jericho clearly demonstrate that God wins our victories by means and principles that look utterly foolish and contradictory to human wisdom. In some of life's situations, God tells us to trust Him, praise Him and watch Him work. All that He requires from us is the step of faith on our part to do what He asks whether we understand it or not. Prayer is an important spiritual weapon to overcome problems, but so is praise. So praise Him, trust Him and watch Him work.

**Father, You are the God of miracles and wonders.
I believe that as I praise You my problems will come
crashing down. Hallelujah!**

THE WAY OF DELIVERANCE

2 Samuel 22:1–20

'I call to the LORD, who is worthy of praise,
and I am saved from my enemies.' (v.4)

The way of praise was, for David, the way of deliverance from his problems. Turn from your problem right now and focus your thoughts on God. With all the sincerity of which you are capable, begin to praise Him. Tell Him how great and wonderful He is, and how glad you are that He is on your side and you on His. Make much of Jesus in your praise, for God delights in His Son. If the devil tells you that this is manipulation, then tell him you will praise God whether He delivers you or not. But mark my words – deliverance will come. The God who lived in David's time is just the same today.

Lord, as I praise You I know I shall step out from the dungeon of despair into the sunshine of victory. Amen.

A PERFECT BALANCE

John 11:17–43

'Then Jesus looked up to heaven and said,
"Father, thank you for hearing me."' (v.41, TLB)

What astonishes me about the miracle of Lazarus returning from the dead, is the apparent ease with which it was performed. There was no great intercessory prayer or a long period of laying hold on God. Jesus simply lifts His eyes to heaven and says, 'Father, thank you for hearing me.' Then He commanded Lazarus to come from the grave – and the man who had been dead for four days walked out! It is my belief that Jesus had done all the praying that was necessary before reaching the tomb, but when He arrived, Jesus used praise as a prelude to a miracle. We too, need a balance of intercessory prayer and praise.

Father, I pray when I ought to be praising, and praise when I ought to be praying. Help me achieve the right balance. Amen.

SENDING PRAISE AHEAD

Mark 6:30–44

'Taking the five loaves and the two fish ...
he gave thanks ...' (v.41)

I have no doubt myself that Jesus used prayer to commune with God and find out what God wanted Him to do in every situation. Then, having prayed, He could approach the situation with confident faith and praise. How did the miracle in our reading occur? Did Jesus plead with God for a supernatural display of His power? No, He looked up to heaven, gave thanks, and the bread extended itself in response to His 'mighty multiplying touch'. It is always right to use prayer as a means of getting to know God's mind on a situation, then once assured of this, we can send praise and thanksgiving ahead in order to bring back the answer.

Father, I see that both prayer and praise are important. Guide me in a right and balanced use of them. For Jesus' sake. Amen.

THE PURPOSE AND POWER OF PRAISE

SINGING JAILBIRDS!

Acts 16:16–34

----

*'And at midnight Paul and Silas prayed,
and sang praises unto God …' (v.25, AV)*

Praise was often used to release God's power into
a dark and difficult situation and turn defeat into
victory. Paul and Silas had a strong, inner conviction that
everything was working out for God's glory and their
good. In such moments it is not necessarily prayer that is
needed but praise. What would have happened, I wonder,
if Paul and Silas had sat in the stocks bemoaning their fate?
I doubt myself if a miracle would have taken place. Praise,
however, became the note around which God constructed a
symphony of sound that broke through the natural barriers
to bring freedom and deliverance to His rejoicing children,
and salvation to others.

**Lord, I see that unutterable peace possesses the hearts
of Your children when they trust and praise You. Amen.**

TRY PRAISE

Psalm 56:1–13

'When I am afraid ... I praise ...' (vv.3–4)

O ne dark period, many years ago, I suffered a few weeks of depression that brought me to the verge of giving up the ministry. I tried praying, but the more I prayed the more depressed I felt. The Spirit said, 'Try praise.' However, I rationalised the issue and persuaded myself that what I was hearing was a voice from my own subconscious. Again the Spirit said, 'Try praise.' I did, and the heaviness lifted from me within seconds. I felt as if a great weight had been taken off my shoulders. Joy flooded into my heart in response to my praise, and from that day to this, serious depression has never once entered my life.

Father, help me to put into practice the truth of what You have been teaching me this past week. For Jesus' sake. Amen.

THE PURPOSE AND POWER OF PRAISE

AN OBEDIENT HEART

Matthew 12:30–37

'… out of the overflow of the heart the mouth speaks.' (v.34)

God's Word spells out a number of conditions and requirements for a thankful worshipper, the first of which is an obedient heart. God considers obedience to His Word more important than extravagant sacrifice. An Old Testament prophet, speaking on behalf of the Almighty, said, 'Behold, to obey is better than sacrifice, and to hearken than the fat of rams' (1 Sam. 15:22). Since 'out of the overflow of the heart the mouth speaks', what we say or sing should reflect the commitment of our hearts to God. If it doesn't, then all our efforts to praise, whether it be by vociferous praise or spectacular music, will fail to reach the ears of our Creator God.

Father, may my praise flow out of a heart that is committed and obedient to You. For Jesus' sake. Amen.

'LOST ON THE WAY UP'

Amos 5:21–24

'Away with the noise of your songs! I will not listen to the music of your harps.' (v.23)

A minister had a dream in which he saw himself standing alongside the throne of God. Although all his congregation were singing, only one voice could be heard in heaven. God explained, 'The only sound that reaches up to heaven is the sound of heartfelt praise – anything less than this is lost on the way up.' In Mark 7:6–7 Jesus quotes the prophet Isaiah, 'These people honour me with their lips, but their hearts are far from me.' Whether our praise is spontaneous or, as with a choir or a singing group, carefully rehearsed and prepared, our sacrifices of thanksgiving and praise must meet God's conditions if they are to be pleasing and acceptable to Him.

Father, enable me to have an obedient heart so that my expressions of thankfulness and praise are not lost on the way up. Amen.

THE PURPOSE AND POWER OF PRAISE

BROKEN RELATIONSHIPS

FOR READING AND MEDITATION

Matthew 5:21–26

*'First go and be reconciled to your brother;
then come and offer your gift.' (v.24)*

Another requirement for a thankful worshipper is reconciliation with fellow Christians. Jesus, in the passage before us today, shows the order of priority in Christian worship. He is saying in effect: 'It's no good coming to God with a sacrifice if you have a broken relationship with a fellow believer. Put that right first and then God will be delighted to accept your offering.' If we fail to take the steps that are necessary to bring about the healing of a broken relationship, then our attempts at worship will never rise higher than the ceiling of the church or room in which we make them.

Father, I cannot praise You when my heart is full of bitterness. Help me to heal any broken relationships I have. Amen.

HUMILITY

Amos 4:1–9

---

*'Bring your sacrifices ... and brag about your
freewill offerings ... this is what you love to do ...'*
(vv.4–5)

A spirit of pride and self-righteousness can make our
sacrifices and thanksgiving unacceptable. It can even
turn an offering of praise into a sinful act. The Pharisee
gave thanks to God that he was not like the tax collector
(Luke 18:9–14). It was thanks that was not really thanks at
all. 'Pride kills thanksgiving,' said Henry Ward Beecher,
'but a humble mind is the soil out of which thanksgiving
naturally grows. A proud man is seldom a grateful man for
he never thinks he gets as much as he deserves.' The most
dangerous parasite I know is spiritual pride – many are
weakened by it and fall in times of testing.

**Father, deliver me, I pray, from the stranglehold that
pride has upon my life. For Jesus' sake. Amen.**

A REJOICING SPIRIT

2 Corinthians 9:6–15; Exodus 35:29

'… for God loves a cheerful giver.' (2 Cor. 9:7)

God loves a cheerful and natural giver, whether it is money or praise they give. Praise that is not given cheerfully falls short of the ideal. When you are given an unwanted Christmas present you grope for words of appreciation that won't come. It was kind of the person to give it to you, of course, and you feel you ought to be grateful, but deep down inside you know it is not real appreciation. However, what happens when you are given something at Christmas you really want? How the words of gratitude tumble out. No feeling that you *ought* to be grateful. You just *are* grateful – you cannot help yourself.

Father, help me to be a truly grateful person, and not engineer gratitude but give the real thing. Amen.

'WITH GRACE'

Colossians 3:16–17; Ephesians 5:18–20

'... singing with grace in your hearts to the Lord.'
(Col. 3:16, NKJV)

What does Paul mean when he says we should praise God 'with grace to the Lord'? The most frequently used word in the New Testament for giving thanks is the Greek word *eucharistein*, which implies intimacy with the person to whom the thanks is given. The root word for thanksgiving is *charis*, 'grace'. Grace is goodwill, magnanimity and large-heartedness. A Christian who has grace will have a generous disposition, will hold no bitterness and harbour no resentment. You can't praise God genuinely if you have a bitter and quarrelsome spirit. If you do then you are praising God without grace in your heart.

Lord, I cannot praise and be at peace with You when my heart is not at peace with others. Help me in Jesus' name. Amen.

THE PURPOSE AND POWER OF PRAISE

FAITH

Hebrews 11:1–10

'... *without faith it is impossible*
to please God ...' (v.6)

Kagawa, the famous Japanese Christian, lost his sight, but faith rose up in him to find a cause for gratitude. He refused to reject or doubt God despite his problems. The real secret of his faith is revealed in his words, 'Despite the lack of my eyesight the whole creation is mine. God threw it in when He gave me Christ.' That is it! All things are ours if we have Christ. As long as I love God and have faith to believe that everything that comes my way can be used for my greater effectiveness, then nothing can stop the swelling of praise in my heart. Nothing.

Father, give me the faith that dares to believe that good comes out of everything when You are in it. Amen.

WORKING WITH GOD'S DESIGN

Psalm 103:1–22

'Praise the LORD, O my soul; all my inmost being, praise his holy name.' (v.1)

What do I do if I don't really feel like praising God? If I give God praise when I don't feel like it, am I not in danger of engineering gratitude? Am I not a hypocrite? Surely, thankfulness is like love; it is only truly satisfying when it is spontaneous. There are three main aspects to our being – will, feelings and thoughts. Our feelings do not respond to an act of will but they are, however, greatly influenced by two other factors – right thinking and right behaviour. Let's begin today by determining to fill our thoughts with the right content, for right thinking always produces right feelings.

Father, help me to feed my thoughts on the message of Your love and Your goodness, then my feelings will carry the message too. Amen.

THINK!

Philippians 4:1–8

'… if anything is … praiseworthy – think about such things.' (v.8)

ur emotions follow our thoughts just like baby ducks follow their mother. Although the will is powerless to influence the emotions, this is not true of the thoughts – thoughts can direct and focus the emotions in a way that can bring about great changes in our feelings. This, then, is the first step on the path of thanksgiving – to think on God's goodness, to fill the mind with the facts concerning His love and to hold them in the thoughts until they, in turn, have their effect on the emotions. Think, therefore, on God's blessings such as salvation, food, good health, clothing and friends, and be thankful.

Father, forgive me for my ingratitude. Help me to focus my thoughts on the abundance of Your blessings. Amen.

NO REASON FOR THANKSGIVING?

2 Corinthians 4:1–15

'... so that the grace that is reaching more and more people may cause thanksgiving to overflow to the glory of God.' (v.15)

In 1930 when America was in depression, the American Association for the Advancement of Atheism raised a strong protest against the keeping of the annual Thanksgiving Day. They claimed that in a country where thousands were without jobs there could be no reason for thanksgiving. Millions, however, ignored their protest and gathered in their homes as usual for Thanksgiving. No reason for thanksgiving? We thank God for the air we breathe, the light by which we see, the kiss of devotion upon the lips of a mother or wife, the cry of a new-born baby, the smell of newly-mown grass. Above all we thank God for Jesus – God with us.

Father, help me to focus more on the sunshine than the shade because You are always with me. Amen.

A JOURNAL OF GRATEFULNESS

Philippians 1:3–11

'I thank my God every time I remember you.' (v.3)

A missionary, who recorded all his prayer requests, claimed that many of his prayers were answered precisely the way he had asked. Whenever he felt discouraged, he would take out his notebook, meditate on the goodness of God to him, and it would not be long before praise would 'bubble up in his soul'. Make a practice of noting God's special blessings to you. Make a practice, too, of thanking those through whom some of God's blessings come. It does people good to be thanked. One man I know keeps a *Journal of Gratefulness* to record the names of those whom God has used to encourage him. He then sends letters of appreciation and thanks.

Father, if there is someone to whom I should say thank you, help me to recall the situation and make contact with them. Amen.

THANKS FOR EVERYTHING

1 Thessalonians 5:16–24

'*... give thanks in all circumstances, for this is God's will for you in Christ Jesus.*' (v.18)

'**P**ride,' says one writer, 'is believing that I achieved what in reality God and others did for me and through me.' Think back as far as you can remember to all the people who have benefited your life. Have you ever thanked them? Make a practice of thanking people even if you have to go to a little trouble to find them. It will please God. He often sends His special mercies by the hands of other people, and He likes His messengers to be thanked also. Gratitude is only as sincere as the effort you make to express it. 'Someone, somewhere, is waiting for a letter from you.'

Lord, make me a thankful person – to both You and Your messengers. Amen.

THE PURPOSE AND POWER OF PRAISE

'A RANSOMED SINNER'

2 Corinthians 9:6–15

'Thank God for his Son – his gift too wonderful for words.' (v.15, TLB)

What is the greatest blessing God has given to us? There can be no doubt about that – it is Christ! A missionary travelling on a plane was given a card with his meal. On the card was written: 'What do you think of our meals?' He wrote: 'Too good for a ransomed sinner.' When the stewardess picked up the card and read it, she smiled and asked him what he meant. He told her that this was the way he looked at everything – not just a meal. He saw everything in the light of being a ransomed sinner. How do you take things – for granted or with gratitude?

Blessed Saviour, I will never get over the wonder of being a ransomed sinner. I shall be grateful for all eternity. Amen.

ACHIEVING THE IMPOSSIBLE

Philippians 2:12–18

'... *God is at work within you, helping you want to obey him, and then helping you do what he wants.*' *(v.13, TLB)*

I once asked a depressed person to read out loud Psalm 136. He did – dolefully. 'Now read it again,' I said, 'but this time throw back your shoulders, say the words with emphasis, and imagine how you would say it if you really believed what you are reading.' He did what I asked and said that immediately he felt better. I got him to read it several times in this way and his depression lifted. There is an important principle here. When we use our wills to do what God asks us to do – praise Him even though we don't feel like it – He responds to this act of faith by bringing about a change in our feelings – miraculously.

Father, give me the faith that believes that when I do the possible, You will do the impossible. Amen.

THE ONE CENTRAL TRUTH

2 Corinthians 2:1–17

'But thanks be to God, who in Christ always leads us in triumph …' (v.14, RSV)

I t is not so much what happens to a Christian that is important, but how he responds to it. We are our responses. When we hit a problem we will most likely take one of four attitudes in attempting to find a solution. We will retreat into the past, escape into the future, withdraw in inner detachment or take everything that comes – good, bad and indifferent – and turn it into something else. Only a Christian can take the last of these ways as only the Christian faith provides the power to turn every difficulty into a discovery, every test into a triumph, every setback into a springboard.

My Father, help me discover the secret of poise and power in the Christian life. In Jesus' name I pray. Amen.

NO LOOKING BACK

Luke 9:57–62

'Jesus replied, "No-one who … looks back is fit for service in the kingdom of God."' (v.62)

T he reason why so many people live in the past is because they have ceased to be creative in the present and retreat into previous success. I spoke to a woman of ninety who took my breath away with the news of what she was doing for the Lord. And not only doing, but planning to do! She was a member of a church I pastored in central London nearly twenty years earlier, but she had little to say about those days. Her mind was fixed very much on the present. Glancing at the past to learn its lessons is wisdom; gazing at the past and trying to live in it is folly.

Father, help me not retreat into the past whenever I am faced with pressing problems. I must live in the present with You. Amen.

FLIGHT INTO THE FUTURE

Acts 1:1–11

"'Men of Galilee," they said, "why do you stand here looking into the sky?"' (v.11)

The opposite of a retreat into the past is a flight into the future. As the present is frustrating, one flies into the future and tries to live there as mental compensation for not being able to handle the present. Such people are the grandiose dreamers who are always going to – but never do. They are the impractical dreamers who don't face the present for they are too busy with the future. The present is messy, the future is glorious – so they try to live in it. They have no roots in the present so they bring forth no fruits in the present. The disciples stopped gazing into the sky and turned the world upside down.

Lord, help me not to look to the future in such a way that it becomes a substitute for facing the issues of the present. Amen.

THE ESCAPE WITHIN

Luke 18:9–14

- - - - - - - - - - - - - - - - - - - -

'To some who were confident of their own righteousness and looked down on everybody else, Jesus told this parable ...' (v.9)

I n detachment we try not to escape into the past or the future, but remain in the present – detached. There are some Christians who, afraid of reality and wanting to compensate for not facing life and its problems, develop a detachment which is apart from the life that surrounds them. They sometimes nurse illusions of grandeur and feelings of superiority in order to compensate for not being involved with others. They may detach themselves from all feelings of concern or love – even love of family. I promise you that if you try to escape within, you won't like the within you escape to – that way is defeatism.

Father, may I face life in reality and not emotionally and physically detach myself from You and others. Amen.

THE WAY OF TRANSFORMATION

Psalm 139:7–12

*'... even there your hand will guide me,
your strength will support me.' (v.10, TLB)*

Reality is dealing with life as it is. The mentally ill find it difficult to face reality, while the mentally healthy face life with calmness and confidence. Life comes to us with many problems – injustice, deceit, pain, hurt, the disloyalty of friends, sickness and so on. For the Christian, however, there is another side to this. Reality includes the sovereignty of God, the loving purposes of the Almighty and the providential care that He has for His own. Reality, for the Christian, is bringing Jesus alongside all of life's problems, seeing life from His point of view and allowing Him to transform us. If you adopt this attitude to life then inevitably you will become a truly praising person.

Father, I am so thankful that I don't need to run away from anything. I can meet everything through You. Amen.

MAKING EVERYTHING SERVE

2 Corinthians 4:7–18

'We are hard pressed … but not crushed … struck down, but not destroyed.' (vv.8–9)

Jesus took the way of reality and transformation. He refused to retreat into Israel's glorious past, refused to escape into the glorious future of the kingdom of God and refused to withdraw in detachment as the Pharisees did. He faced life realistically, took everything in His hands and transformed it to serve Him. He worked as a lowly carpenter without complaint. He met temptation in the wilderness and made it strengthen Him. He went into the wilderness 'full of the Holy Spirit' and came out 'in the power of the Spirit' (Luke 4:1,14). Temptation turned fullness into power. He transformed twelve ordinary men into preachers who changed the course of history. He transforms us still.

Father, with You I can transform everything that comes, so praise will be as natural to me as the very air I breathe. Amen.

THE PURPOSE AND POWER OF PRAISE

A RADIANT PHILOSOPHY

Hebrews 13:1–8

'For God has said, "I will never ... fail you nor forsake you." That is why we can say ... "The Lord is my helper and I am not afraid of anything ..."'
(vv.5–6, TLB)

A Christian can face all the adversities of life triumphantly because he knows it is not so much what happens to us that is important but how we respond to it. A New Testament text referring to Joseph says: 'And the patriarchs, jealous of Joseph, sold him into Egypt; but God ...' (Acts 7:9, RSV). That phrase, 'But God' is at the end of every injustice and every problem – He has the last word. Christ can transform every bad thing that comes your way – sorrow, pain, hurt, disloyalty, bereavement – everything, providing you let Him. This is an incomparable philosophy of life – and a radiant one.

Lord, I can face everything in the knowledge that life can do nothing to me that You cannot transform for Your purpose. Amen.

REDEMPTIVE REACTIONS

Luke 10:25–37

'On one occasion an expert in the law stood up to test Jesus.' (v.25)

The actions of Jesus were wonderful, but so were His reactions. About half the Gospels are taken up with a description of His actions and the other half with His reactions. And His reactions were as redemptive and as revealing as His actions. When a lawyer stood up to put Him to the test, He answered his question and then gave the world the unforgettable story of the Good Samaritan. On the cross, He prayed, 'Father, forgive them; for they know not what they do' (Luke 23:34). The highest reaction to the greatest injustice. That reaction revealed the nature of God as redemptive love in final terms.

Lord Jesus, help me to react redemptively to everything that comes my way so I reveal more of You. Amen.

TURNING HELL INTO HEAVEN

1 Corinthians 13:1–13

'Love never fails ...' (v.8)

Right reactions are equally as important as right actions. A Christian woman considered divorcing her abusive husband. Instead she prayed every day, 'Lord, teach me how to respond in this situation so that I might make this problem serve the ends of Your kingdom.' She continued to show such love to her husband that eventually her love broke him. He gave his life to Jesus Christ, stopped drinking and rebuilt his business. The daughter said to her mother, 'If that had been me I doubt whether I could have done it.' But the mother, by utilising the grace God gave her and reacting in a loving way, succeeded in turning a hell into a heaven.

Father, there is a great gap between what I am and what I know I can be. Help me to close that gap. Amen.

UNRESOLVED CONFLICTS

Luke 9:51–56

----

*'When the disciples ... saw this, they asked,
"Lord, do you want us to call fire down from
heaven to destroy them?"' (v.54)*

I n this world a Christian is bound to be treated un-
Christianly, for humanity is largely un-Christian. The
reactions to un-Christian treatment become as important
as our actions. I knew a woman who, because her family
were treating her in an un-Christian way, developed a
good deal of self-pity which pushed her toward a martyr
complex. She saw how much she was drifting from the
Christian position and surrendered her attitude of self-pity.
When our problems of inferiority, resentment, self-pity
and so on are surrendered to God, and we receive His
grace, we can become transformed into the image of His
dear Son.

**Father, from today, and by Your grace, I shall no longer
play nursemaid to any resentment or wrong reaction.
Help me, Lord Jesus. Amen.**

A LADDER TO RIGHT REACTIONS

Romans 12:9–21

'Do not be overcome by evil, but overcome evil with good.' (v.21)

It is possible to climb out of the pit of distorted thinking and wrong reactions. First, spend some time quietly before God going over your life to see if you are reacting wrongly to life's situations. Second, be alert to the fact that you will try to defend yourself since defences have been built up by you over many years to justify your reactions. Many of us argue ourselves into self-justification of our reactions so that it is not easy to admit we are wrong. It is far easier to confess wrong actions than wrong reactions. So pay special attention to this, for unless you win here you will be blocked all along the way.

Lord Jesus, save me completely from wrong reactions and wrong actions. I surrender both to You now. Amen.

LIKE PRODUCES LIKE

Mark 3:20–30

'... How can Satan drive out Satan?' (v.23)

Be relentless with your wrong reactions, uproot them, get them out, leave no roots to sprout again. It's no good chopping away at the trunk or the branches if the roots are allowed to remain. Resentment of others will only succeed in more resentment. Can Satan cast out Satan? Can you, by acting like the devil, get the devil out of people? Like produces like: a bitter spring produces a bitter stream, and resentment produces resentment. Dig remorselessly into your life and make sure that everything is brought up and out. A partial surrender ends only in a whole defeat.

Lord, I want to take a step once and for all away from wrong reactions to right reactions. For Jesus' sake. Amen.

THE PURPOSE AND POWER OF PRAISE

BE READY TO CHANGE

Philippians 3:1–11

'… whatever was to my profit I now consider loss for the sake of Christ.' (v.7)

esist the built-in desire you have to stay as you are, and make up your mind that with God's help you are going to change. There is something about human nature that resists change. We cling to old habits and desires simply because, like shoes we have worn for some time, they feel comfortable and secure. Our ability and willingness to change for the better into Christlikeness, however, determines our spiritual poise and power. At the heart of many lives is a worm eating away that says 'Suppose this is taken away or lost or destroyed – what then?' Imagine that happening and then respond with praise because you will still have God.

O Father, in You I am safe, for nothing can work successfully against me. Eternal praise be to Your name. Amen.

'IT COMES TO PASS'

Psalm 30:1–12

'... *weeping may remain for a night, but rejoicing comes in the morning.' (v.5)*

Accept God's forgiveness for your wrong reactions as well as for your wrong actions. God is as eager to deliver you from your wrong reactions as from your wrong actions. The father in the story of the prodigal son was willing to restore his younger son who had sinned by his actions, but he was just as eager to restore the elder son who had sinned by his wrong reactions of bitterness and unforgiveness. Realise that everything that comes, comes to pass. Hold on to God and ride out the storm. It has come – but it has come to pass. The sorrow comes and passes, but the joy goes on for ever.

Father, I am thankful that my temporary light afflictions are working out for me 'an eternal glory that far outweighs them all' (2 Cor. 4:17). Amen.

PRAISE THE LORD

Romans 12:9–21

'Rejoice with those who rejoice, weep with those who weep.' (v.15, RSV)

L et us be on our guard that we do not reduce praise to the level of mere clichés. 'Praise the Lord' is a wonderful phrase but may be inappropriate if said to bereaved parents. What makes Christians turn such phrases into clichés? The main reason is because they lack a deep faith in the providence of God, and so they try to reassure themselves by the use of nice-sounding phrases. It is a form of escapism which seeks to dull the harshness of reality. One Christian psychiatrist refers to it as a form of Christian schizophrenia – a faith that maintains itself by means of a fantasy world, completely divorced from the real world of pain, suffering, evil and a cross.

Father, make me sensitive to the hurts and suffering of others so that I do not gloss over their problems. Amen.

WHY JESUS WEPT

John 11:17–44

'Jesus wept.' (v.35)

One of the reasons Jesus wept, in my opinion, is because He felt keenly the pain and grief that filled the hearts of Mary and Martha. The natural consequence of empathy is often the shedding of tears. Empathy, by the way, has been described as 'your pain in my heart'. When you can weep with someone who is facing a tragedy, when you can take their pain into your heart, when you can empathise with their hurt and anguish, then, and only then, have you earned the right to say to that person, 'Let us give thanks and praise to the Lord'. Let us be sensitive to others when we praise God.

Father, help me to be sensitive to others and so earn the right to point them to a new way of living. Amen.

THE PURPOSE AND POWER OF PRAISE

BE YOURSELF

Philippians 2:1–11

'Do nothing out of selfish ambition or vain conceit ...' (v.3)

We can use praise for personal gains. A man said, 'All my life I have suffered with an inferiority complex, and I can see that when I am praying to God, particularly when I am praising Him in a group, I love to use extravagant language because it makes me feel good – it boosts my flagging ego.' We must guard against taking something as beautiful as praise and making it serve our ends rather than God's. When praising God you don't have to put on airs and graces, adopt a special tone of voice or engage in language and phrases that are not a natural part of your personality. Don't pretend to be more than you are – be yourself.

Father, save me from myself. Help me to be free of any hindrances – free to be myself. Amen.

DON'T BARGAIN WITH GOD

FOR READING AND MEDITATION
Psalm 47:1–9

'Sing praises with understanding.' (v.7, NKJV)

We must use praise as appreciation not manipulation. Praise is not a bargaining position. We must not adopt the attitude, 'Well, Lord, I'm going to praise you because, if I don't, I know you won't bless me.' To praise God is to delight in Him. What does it mean to praise with understanding? It means understanding the fact that although we cannot sometimes fathom why God does certain things, or permits situations to develop in our lives, nevertheless, He permits only what He can use. This is the basis for praise. We must understand that God loves us and has a perfect plan for our lives, whatever the appearances to the contrary.

Father, I understand that You only permit what You can use, and that You truly love and care for me. Amen.

THE PURPOSE AND POWER OF PRAISE

WE ARE FREE!

1 John 4:7–21

'This is love: not that we loved God, but that he loved us …' (v.10)

Some Christians regard praise as earning God's approval. God does not love us because we are thankful, rather we are thankful because He loves us. He doesn't need our thanks. We are free! God's attitude toward us is the same – love – no matter what our attitude or response to Him may be. Your thankfulness certainly changes you so that you can receive more of that love, but the block is never in Him – it is in you. Because we are free to be thankful, this presents us with a uniquely human possibility – the choice to respond to Him spontaneously in thankfulness. Genuine thanks are freely given. How could they be genuine if they were conditional or coerced?

Father, thank You that I am free to praise for no other motive than I want to because of Your love for me. Amen.

NOT ENOUGH STARS!

FOR READING AND MEDITATION

Psalm 145:1–21

*'Great is the LORD and most worthy
of praise ...' (v.3)*

What endless reasons we have to be thankful! A young
girl with a disability said, 'I pick out the brightest
star I can find at night and I say, "That's for Mummy." I
pick out another one and say, "That's for Daddy." I find
a twinkling one for my brother, my puppy, my doctor,
my spinal perambulator ...' On and on she went. Her list
seemed endless and some time later, when she appeared
to be running out of breath, she said, 'But there just aren't
enough stars to go round.' If you think you have no reasons
to be thankful, then look out tonight and count the stars.
There aren't enough stars to go round.

**O God, You have given me so much: give me one thing
more – a praising heart. For Jesus' sake I ask it. Amen.**

THE PURPOSE AND POWER OF PRAISE

SEPTEMBER 1
'LIKE A JACOB'

1 Corinthians 10:1–13

'These things happened to them as examples and were written down as warnings for us ...' (v.11)

Why does the Bible contain so many biographies? The answer came in the words of the text which is before us today. Incidents in the lives of certain men and women who lived in Bible days have been recorded for us by the Holy Spirit so that as we examine them we might learn from both their failures and their successes. Every important biblical principle is illustrated in the lives of the men and women recorded in the Scriptures. For example, Jacob was a cheat, a supplanter and a crook. Jeremiah said of him: '... for a brother will cheat like a Jacob' (Jer. 9:4, Moffatt). Bible characters reveal the bad to avoid as well as the good to emulate.

Father, teach me how to live a life of faith through the records of those who have gone before. Amen.

THE ROOT OF SIN

Genesis 25:19–34

'Jacob said, "First sell me your birthright."'
(v.31, RSV)

When God faded out, then Jacob made himself God. He became a self-centred man – the centre of his universe. He began to look at things in relation to himself – how he would benefit and how he would prosper. The root of sin, as I have said time and time again, is self-centredness. We are not designed to function with self at the centre. God designed us so that He might be at the centre of our lives, and when He is, then life runs harmoniously – in tune with God and the universe. If we live this way – with God at the centre – we get results. If we live any other way, we get consequences.

Father, I must be a God-centred and not a self-centred person. Help me to make the adjustment – today. Amen.

THE LAST WORD

Genesis 27:5–41

'Esau said, "Is he not rightly named Jacob? For he has supplanted me these two times."'(v.36, RSV)

In this God-designed universe, no one breaks a moral law and gets away with it. They may appear to do so, but in reality they reap the consequences. Jacob got what he wanted, but he also got something else – 'Esau hated Jacob' (v.41). He got his way, plus the hatred of Esau. We reap what we sow – inevitably. People who are always complaining about others are simply revealing their own inner discontent with themselves. The consequence of doing wrong is being the one who does the wrong. 'My trouble,' said a well-known philosopher, 'is that I go everywhere I go.' A moral universe always has the last word – you can't run away from yourself.

Father, I can't cheat a moral universe – it will get me in the end. Help me to stop trying. Amen.

REAPING WHAT WE SOW

Genesis 29:1–30

'So Jacob served seven years for Rachel ...
because of the love he had for her.' (v.20, RSV)

Jacob soon began to scheme to get his hands on his father-in-law's property. He worked out a plan so that the weaker lambs fell to Laban and the stronger ones went to himself (Gen. 30:35–42). He was still Jacob – the man who would use any method to further self-interest. Once again he got what he wanted, plus the consequences. And what were the consequences? The ill will of Laban and his sons. 'Jacob learned that Laban's sons were grumbling ... Soon Jacob noticed a considerable cooling in Laban's attitude towards him' (Gen. 31:1–2, TLB). We cannot alter a moral law. We reap what we sow – inevitably.

Father, thank You for reminding me that if I try to cheat, then first and foremost I cheat myself. Amen.

NOT 'WHAT' BUT 'WHO'

Genesis 31:17–31

'And Jacob outwitted Laban … in that he did not tell him that he intended to flee.' (v.20, RSV)

Jacob found that by running away from Laban, he was running into Esau (Gen. 32:6). Having created two difficult situations by his trickery, he was now caught between them. In such a situation there is only one place to run – into the arms of a loving and forgiving God. However, Jacob prays to be saved from the consequences of his sin, rather than from the sin itself – the sin of self-centredness. He wasn't ready for deliverance yet because he was still pointing to his circumstances as his problem, while his main problem was himself. In most circumstances, the question is not 'what' is wrong, but 'who' is wrong.

Father, I am so prone to blaming this, that and the other instead of pointing to myself. Forgive me. For Jesus' sake. Amen.

'WHAT IS YOUR NAME?'

Genesis 32:1–27

'And he said to him, "What is your name?"'
(v.27, RSV)

Jacob is near to rock bottom. Despite his clever strategies, he was unable to dodge the consequences, and we read that he was 'frantic with fear' (v.7, TLB). He had no way out; except God's way. 'What is your name?' asks the divine wrestler. It seems an innocent and almost unnecessary question, but in Bible times names were not just designations, they were definitions. A name was an expression of character. Jacob confesses, 'I am Jacob' – the supplanter. Now the depths were uncovered. His soul was naked before God. The real man was up and out. This was the moment of truth. In confessing his name, he confessed his problem. The game was up.

O God, the game is up. Save me from myself and take over the central place in my being. Amen.

JACOB DEAD — ISRAEL ALIVE!

Genesis 32:28–33:20

'Then he said, "Your name shall no more be called Jacob, but Israel ..."' (32:28, RSV)

What is your name? I don't mean the name you were given at birth, but the name that best describes your personality. Perhaps your name is 'Fear' – it cripples your whole being. Perhaps it is 'Ego', 'Self-pity', 'Pride', 'Hypocrisy' or 'Guilt'. There can be no new name until you confess the old name. When Jacob confessed his old name, the angel gave him a new one – Israel. Jacob's new name meant 'one who has power with God' (TLB). Jacob was dead, but Israel was alive! How true it is that when something happens inside us, something happens outside us. A changed Jacob made a changed Esau. Jacob's complete dedication to God resulted in a moral and spiritual revival (Gen. 35:2-4).

O God, change others by changing me. Change my name, my character, my influence – today. In Jesus' name. Amen.

GOD'S DUAL VISION

Judges 6:1–16

'... *Gideon was beating out wheat in the wine press, to hide it from the Midianites.*' *(v.11, RSV)*

G ideon is a somewhat sorry figure – his mood of fear and self-pity epitomising that of the whole nation of Israel. Gideon threshes wheat in the wine press to hide it from the Midianites – the picture being one of timidity, hesitancy and concealment. The angel of the Lord addresses Gideon with the salutation: 'The Lord is with you, you mighty man of valour ...' God sees us not as we are, but as we can be. He has dual vision. How did God know that Gideon the daring was in Gideon the disconsolate? How did God know that Peter the rock was in Peter the unstable? Because He has dual vision and sees the inwardness of things.

Father, help me to remember that You see me not as I am, but as I can be. Thank You, Lord. Amen.

THE GOD WHO IS ALIVE

FOR READING AND MEDITATION

Judges 6:17–35

'... Gideon said, "Alas, O Lord God! For now I have seen the angel of the Lord face to face."' (v.22, RSV)

What turned Gideon from a fearful and dispirited personality into such a mighty man of valour? It was not just the miraculous visitation of the angel but the knowledge that God was living and active and ready to work on behalf of His people. Our faith must never be in miracles, but in the God of miracles. Some plead for miracles simply to meet some deep, inner need of their personality, but miracles ought to be the result, not the cause, of our faith. Let's focus our eyes once more on our God who is alive, active and reigning. The gaze of faith can, yet again, bring down God's supernatural power from heaven to earth.

Father help me to show the fact that You are not merely alive – but alive in me. For Jesus' sake. Amen.

THE SIGN OF THE FLEECE

FOR READING AND MEDITATION

Judges 6:36–40

'Then Gideon said to God, "If you are really going to use me to save Israel as you promised, prove it to me in this way ..."' (vv.36–37, TLB)

There are many who criticise Gideon saying that he should have been content with the sign from the angel. I agree that it is a pattern we ought not to follow, but consider Gideon's position and circumstances for a moment. Hard-pressed by the Midianites, living from day to day in fear of his life and demoralised by what had happened to the once great nation of Israel, Gideon can be forgiven for desiring the issue to be reconfirmed. How reassuring it is for us, when overcome by a sense of worthlessness and inadequacy, to know that when we are unsure of God's call, He is willing to accommodate our frailty and speak, yet again, to our hearts.

Father, thank You for Your patient understanding of my human weakness and frailty. In Jesus' name I pray. Amen.

THE RIGHT PEOPLE

Judges 7:1–8

"'I'll conquer the Midianites with these three hundred,' the Lord told Gideon. "Send all the others home!'" (v.7, TLB)

Whenever God seeks to bring about a change in a society or in a nation, He usually does three things: He looks for the right people, gives them the right plan and puts them in the right place. In directing Gideon to find the right people for his army, the Lord appointed two tests. The first was a test of fearfulness. The second test was a test of faithfulness. Today, as in Gideon's day, the Lord is building an army to rout Satan and his forces, and those who want to be on the front line of battle are given a similar test. God is asking: Are you ready for a tough battle with the enemy?

Father, help me to drink of Your Spirit, not simply for personal refreshment, but for more effective service. For Jesus' sake. Amen.

THE RIGHT PLAN

Judges 7:9–20

'They blew their trumpets and broke the jars that were in their hands.' (v.19)

The plan God gave Gideon for overcoming the enemy consisted of three things – lights, jars and trumpets. How does this divine plan relate to us at this present time? The light speaks of brightness, the shattered jars speak of brokenness and the trumpets speak of boldness. Inside each one of us God has placed the light of His presence, but we must be prepared to have our own self-interests broken and shattered so that self dies and God's power shows through. The trumpet speaks of boldness – the boldness of faith that takes its stand on God's Word, and says, as did Luther, 'Here I stand. I can do no other.'

Father, break me, mould me, fill me and sweep through my life today so that all Your purposes for me shall be realised. Amen.

BIBLE BIOGRAPHIES

THE RIGHT PLACE

Judges 7:21–25

'They stood every man in his place ...' (v.21, RSV)

As each man took up his appointed place, and stood exactly where he was positioned by Gideon, the Lord was able to bring about a mighty victory. For God's purposes to come to pass in our lives, it is imperative that we stay or move into the place God has appointed for us. God has designed us to fulfil a distinct purpose in His Body, the Church, and if we don't fit into His plans for us, then we greatly affect its smooth functioning. Take up the challenge and ask God if you are functioning in the role for which God has specifically equipped you.

Father, show me the ministry You have chosen to give me, and the place You want me to be. Amen.

WHEN GOD AND MAN MAKE CONTACT

Judges 8:1–23

'... *the* LORD *will rule over you.*' (v.23, RSV)

S tudying biblical biographies leaves us without excuse, for, by the side of these men and women, who amongst us can plead that we are too inadequate, too worthless or too insignificant? The main lesson of Gideon's life is that God is able to confer upon the most timid spirit a boldness that is utterly beyond the power of the imagination to conceive. Who would have believed that the fearful, timid and insecure Gideon could have led his people into a great and mighty victory? When God and a human being make contact, history is at a turning point. Let Gideon's life motivate you to some new project for God.

Father, touch my life in the way that You touched Gideon's, and fill me with a divine boldness. In Jesus' name. Amen.

SPIRITUAL DESPERATION

1 Samuel 1:1–20

'She named him Samuel, saying, "Because I asked the LORD for him."' (v.20)

Samuel was the son of a praying mother, and the child of answered prayer. His very name means 'one asked of God'. So intense was Hannah's praying in the Temple that Eli, the priest, thought she was drunk. How many of our prayers go unanswered, I wonder, because we never get desperate enough to lay hold on God and pray through to complete victory? I am convinced that there is a level of prayer that few of us reach because we never get quite desperate enough about the issues. 'You can never understand prayer or the Bible aright,' said a famous theologian, 'until you approach them as a desperate man.'

Lord, put within my heart a holy desperation that will drive me to new heights of prayer and spiritual power. Amen.

BASIC NEEDS OF CHILDREN

1 Samuel 1:21–28

'So the woman stayed at home and nursed her son until she had weaned him.' (v.23)

Children, if they are to grow up with healthy personalities, need three basic things: (1) a sense of belonging (or being loved), (2) a sense of worth (or feeling of value) and (3) a sense of being able to contribute (a sense of purpose). Studies have shown that if these needs are not met, then the door is open to all kinds of problems. As Hannah and Elkanah spent time with Samuel, the growing child no doubt became aware that he was loved and valued. As Samuel begins to assist Eli in the Temple, and is given responsibility, a sense of purpose develops within him. He is on course for a good and godly life.

Father, help parents meet the basic needs of their children so that they develop into healthy adults. Amen.

SAMUEL BECOMES A PROPHET

FOR READING AND MEDITATION
1 Samuel 3:1–18

'Then Eli realised that the LORD was calling the boy.' (v.8)

One night Samuel receives a direct communication from the Lord. He hears his name called and, thinking it to be Eli's voice, he runs to him in obedience. Eli says that he has not called, and Samuel returns to his bed. Three times this happens. Finally, Eli realises that it is the Lord, and he tells Samuel what to do. Samuel eventually tells Eli that God had marked out the old priest's sons for judgment. The significance of this revelation is not so much what will happen to Eli's sons, but that it openly attests, from this moment, that Samuel is a prophet of the Lord.

O Lord, help me to recognise Your voice when it speaks to me, that I may speak for You. Amen.

'EBENEZER'

FOR READING AND MEDITATION

1 Samuel 7:2–13

'He named it Ebenezer, saying,
"Thus far has the LORD helped us."' (v.12)

S amuel commemorates a great victory by erecting a pillar which he calls Ebenezer: 'Thus far has the LORD helped us.' This was a pillar of reminder and gratitude for God's deliverance and blessing. It is fitting that God's mercies and benefits should be acknowledged with thanksgiving. How sad that we so often forget to praise Him for His goodness to us. Has God done something special for you in the past few days or weeks, and you have not yet raised an 'Ebenezer' to Him? Then do so today. Remember, you never really receive a blessing until you are grateful for it.

Father, may I always return thanks for the blessings You have showered upon me. In Jesus' name. Amen.

COPING WITH REJECTION

FOR READING AND MEDITATION
1 Samuel 8:1–22

- -

'… it is not you they have rejected, but they have rejected me as their king.' (v.7)

Have you ever been rejected? It hurts, doesn't it? In overcoming rejection, follow Samuel's procedure. First, he lays the matter before the Lord (v.6). This is always the first step to take when feeling rejected – talk to God about it. Tell Him exactly how you feel and why. This will keep you from harbouring resentment. Second, Samuel willingly submits himself to God's directions. Third, Samuel faced the issue, and patiently bore the people's ingratitude. God was with Samuel in his moment of rejection just as He is with you right now. He will never abandon you or desert you. He is with you – every step of the way.

Lord, You knew so deeply the pain of rejection, and yet made it serve Your purposes. Teach me the selfsame art. Amen.

WALKING WITH DESTINY

FOR READING AND MEDITATION

1 Samuel 9:1–10:1

'When Samuel caught sight of Saul, the LORD said to him, "This is the man ... he will govern my people."' (9:17)

It is impossible to read this account without seeing how beautifully all events are controlled by God. This is not to say, however, that we are mere puppets in the hands of a Master Puppeteer. Each person acts in complete freedom, but God intervenes to work out everything according to His purposes. Was it coincidental that Saul arrived in Ramah on the very day Samuel had just returned there (vv.12–13)? Be encouraged by God's unseen involvement in your earthly affairs. A 'chance' meeting, a 'delayed' letter, a 'missed' appointment are often part of His providential purposes to turn the good into better, and the better into best.

Father, thank You for the providence that works in my life towards positive and fruitful ends. In Jesus' name. Amen.

LOYALTY UNDER TEST

1 Samuel 15:10–35

'Saul replied, "I have sinned. But please honour
me ..." So Samuel went back with Saul ...'
(vv.30–31)

Although Samuel knew the policy of seeking a king was
wrong, and although his own counsel was discarded
and his own position compromised, he refuses to desert his
task or to give way to self-pity and scorn. Fidelity to God
and to His people held him steadfastly on course. It is only
in the context of disagreement, defeat and rejection that
the quality of loyalty is revealed. When our point of view is
ignored, our warnings disregarded and the path we think
best is not followed, to share in spiritual fellowship with
those who differ from us with even greater diligence and
dedication – that is loyalty indeed.

**Father, help me so my life, too, shall be stamped with
the qualities of integrity and loyalty. For Jesus' sake.
Amen.**

DIVINE SOVEREIGNTY

FOR READING AND MEDITATION
1 Samuel 14:20–45

'So the men rescued Jonathan, and he was not put to death.' (v.45)

Jonathan, unaware of Saul's command, eats some honey. In giving the order for his son to be put to death, Saul succeeds only in alienating his men. They stubbornly refuse to obey him. The providence of God surrounded Jonathan, just as it surrounds you and me. God would not permit Jonathan's life to be brought to an end before His purposes for him were fulfilled, and that same principle applies to your life and mine. God has a purpose for each one of us in His kingdom, and He is sovereignly at work superintending the events of our lives, to ensure that His purposes for us are not defeated or overthrown.

O God, I see that I needlessly burden myself when I fail to focus on Your sovereignty. Help me to see that nothing can happen to me other than that which Your love appoints. Amen.

TRUE FRIENDSHIP

1 Samuel 18:1–5

'... *Jonathan became one in spirit with David,
and he loved him as himself.' (v.1)*

Jonathan sensed in David a soul that was honest and
sincere, whereupon he made a covenant with him
based on respect, compatibility and shared ideals. It is
one of the signs of the times that few people are able to
develop such a degree of friendship as is seen here. David
Reisman claims that since World War II a great change has
taken place in society, in which friendships are no longer
deep but superficial. True friendship, as with David and
Jonathan, is a deep committed relationship. It reinforces
us as we face the struggles and ups and downs of life and
rejoices in our successes without any sign of jealousy.

**Father, help me experience the joys of true friendship –
not merely to have a friend, but to be a friend. Amen.**

THE VOICE OF EXPEDIENCY

1 Samuel 19:1–7

*'Jonathan spoke well of David to Saul
his father ...' (v.4)*

Saul became extremely jealous of David, and openly began to plan his assassination. It was at this point that Jonathan demonstrated his deep regard and affection for David by taking up the position as David's mediator. As soon as Jonathan learns of his father's evil intentions, he warns David of the imminent danger facing him, and then, in turn, approaches his father to intercede on David's behalf. Jonathan's sensitive handling of the situation shows the extent to which he is guided by deep, inner principles despite danger to himself. Today we have a phrase, 'look after No. 1'. This is the voice of expediency, and I beg you not to heed it.

Father, help me in every difficult situation to be guided by principle and not by expediency, and be a true friend. Amen.

NO COMPROMISE

FOR READING AND MEDITATION

1 Samuel 19:8–18; 20:1–4

'Jonathan said to David, "Whatever you want me to do, I'll do for you."' (20:4)

I n David's attitude, we catch a glimpse of one of the characteristics of true friendship – vulnerability. David opens up his heart to Jonathan, and exposes his motives and conduct to his friend for evaluation. He feels very secure in Jonathan's presence, and is confident that he can trust him with his most intimate thoughts. Actually, in David, Jonathan has his most formidable rival because the throne belonged to him by right of succession. To befriend David is to offend his father and jeopardise his personal interests. Jonathan would not compromise his friendship, no matter how it affected his personal interests, and neither should we.

Father, give to me the inner fortitude to face all situations courageously, and to act rightly and decisively in all things. Amen.

THE PRINCIPLES OF ENCOURAGEMENT

FOR READING AND MEDITATION
1 Samuel 20:5–42

'Jonathan said to David, "Go in peace, for we have sworn friendship with each other …"' (v.42)

Sensing, as he talks to him, that David is greatly discouraged, Jonathan seeks to encourage him in the Lord: 'Don't be afraid. My father Saul will not lay a hand on you. You shall be king over Israel.' A Christian psychologist says these words contain three principles to help those who are discouraged. Jonathan helped David to identify his problem of fear – 'Don't be afraid.' Jonathan reminded David of God's providential care – 'My father Saul will not lay a hand on you.' Finally, Jonathan focused David's thoughts on God's unalterable promise – 'You shall be king over Israel.' God is with us, God cares for us, and what God has promised, He will perform.

O Father, put me in touch with someone who needs a word of encouragement, and use me, I pray. Amen.

UNFAILING LOVE

FOR READING AND MEDITATION
2 Samuel 1:17–26

'… your love to me was wonderful …' (v.26, RSV)

Consider Jonathan's love for David. In making a covenant, Jonathan had stripped himself of every symbol of royalty in favour of the young shepherd boy. When David's faith was on the point of faltering, and he might have given up altogether, Jonathan went to him and strengthened his hand in God. Jonathan's love for David was not only great in its character but also great in its consistency. In the face of opposition from his father, Jonathan took David's side and remained his loyal friend. What sort of friend are you? Are you trustworthy, steadfast, reliable, loyal and sure? Ask God's help in making you what Jonathan was to David – 'a friend who sticks closer than a brother'.

Father, help me live out the principles of friendship so that I can be the visible form of Your love to others. Amen.

A GREATER THAN JONATHAN

FOR READING AND MEDITATION

2 Samuel 1:23–26; 1 John 4:7–16

'Beloved, let us love one another ...'
(1 John 4:7, RSV)

Beautiful and dramatic though the love of Jonathan was for David, it pales into insignificance compared to our Lord's love for us. Sit at the foot of the cross with me for a moment and contemplate the love of Christ. Look at that thorn-crowned brow, look at the crucified hands and feet, gaze at the open side, the blood in His hair and beard, the spittle of the soldier upon His cheek. Think of it! This is the Lord of glory, the Prince of heaven, the Ruler of the universe. Jonathan's stripping of his robes, and divesting himself of the symbols of royalty, are as nothing compared with this. Christ's love to us is wonderful.

Lord, Your net of love has drawn the hearts and minds of multitudes to the shore of Your purposes. Thank You I am one. Amen.

HE'S ALIVE!

FOR READING AND MEDITATION
1 Kings 16:21–17:1

'Then Elijah ... told King Ahab, "As surely as the Lord God of Israel lives ..."' (17:1, TLB)

I n the midst of spiritual decline, Elijah takes a stand for truth and righteousness. We ask ourselves: from where did such courage come? Firstly, Elijah was convinced that God was not dead but marvellously alive: 'As surely as the Lord God of Israel lives ...' One man convinced that God was alive turned a morally bankrupt nation back to God. What is going on in our experience that is proof positive of the reality of a God who is alive? The world is not impressed by our intellectual arguments; it will be impressed only when it sees the power of God at work in our human life and experience.

O God, help me not only to tell people You are alive, but to show them – by Your life in me. Amen.

HIS PERSONAL REPRESENTATIVE

FOR READING AND MEDITATION

1 Kings 17:1–5

'... the God whom I worship and serve ...' (v.1, TLB)

Elijah's courage was also due to the fact that he knew he was a personal representative of God. You and I are personal representatives of the living God in the day and age in which we live. Whether you stand in a pulpit, a classroom, an office, a factory or a home, if you belong to Christ then you are His personal representative to the world. He wants to change things – through you. Another factor that gave a sharp cutting edge to Elijah's convictions was the fact that he knew God heard and answered prayer. We have the same resources as Elijah – the Word of God, the promise of God and the way of prayer.

Father, thank You for Your Word, Your promises and Your willingness to answer prayer. May I represent You powerfully. Amen.

ELIJAH IN CONCEALMENT

1 Kings 17:1–7

'Then the Lord said to Elijah, "Go ... and hide ..."'
(vv.2–3, TLB)

One of the secrets of success in the Christian life is to be as ready to obey God's voice when He directs us into inaction as we are when He leads us into action. I am persuaded in my own mind that there are many Christians today to whom God is saying, 'Go ... and hide', but they fail to obey because inwardly they are compulsive activists, and regard themselves as worthwhile only when they are doing something, saying something or involved in some 'important' project. In the final analysis, the important thing is not so much what you are doing, but whether what you are doing is the thing God has directed you to do.

Father, help me to clearly hear Your voice so I understand Your directions and obey them. For Jesus' sake. Amen.

GOD IS NO MAN'S DEBTOR

1 Kings 17:8–16

----

*'For no matter how much they used,
there was always plenty left ...' (v.16, TLB)*

Elijah's request to have the first portion of that meal
may seem, on the surface, to be extremely selfish, but
here God is illustrating a divine principle which is later
taken up and expanded in the New Testament: 'Give, and it
will be given to you' (Luke 6:38). When we give to God out
of our meagre supply, we make it possible for God to give
back to us 'a good measure, pressed down, shaken together
and running over'. Obeying the prophet's command,
the woman found this action to be the beginning of a
miraculous supply. Let the truth be written in letters of fire
on every heart: God is no man's debtor.

**Father, I too often wait until I have received before I
give. Teach me to give before I receive. Amen.**

'THE BATTLE OF THE GODS'

1 Kings 18:20–40

'Then the fire of the LORD fell and burned up the sacrifice ... and also licked up the water ...' (v.38)

This story has been described by someone as 'the battle of the gods'. Baal was the chief deity of the Canaanites and regarded as the god of fire. The message from Elijah's experience on Mount Carmel is this – one person with God is always a majority. Divine mathematics is quite distinct from human mathematics. Four hundred and fifty to one – isn't that formidable odds? But that's not the equation. It is four hundred and fifty to one – plus God. We are so often impressed by numbers, but God is not. We delight to add, but God delights to multiply. In any age, a believer who is truly joined to God constitutes a distinct majority.

Father, whoever or whatever is against me, when I am one with You and Your purposes, I am in the majority. Amen.

'GOD DOES NOTHING BUT BY PRAYER'

FOR READING AND MEDITATION

1 Kings 18:41–46

'… there is the sound of a heavy rain.' (v.41)

Several characteristics of Elijah's prayer life are worth noting. Firstly, he was faithful in prayer. If God promised to send rain, then why pray? The answer is because prayer lays down the rails along which God's power can travel to change situations. Wesley said, 'God does nothing but by prayer.' God's plans need our prayers as the bridge over which divine blessings pass. Secondly, Elijah was expectant in prayer. He heard rain when there was not a single cloud in the sky. The ear of faith can hear when the natural eye cannot see. Thirdly, Elijah prayed continuously and earnestly until the answer came (see James 5:17).

Father, help me to strengthen my prayer life, so that I can be a bridge over which Your blessings pass. Amen.

BIBLE BIOGRAPHIES

ELIJAH IN DEPRESSION

1 Kings 19:1–21

'… as he was sleeping, an angel touched him and told him to get up and eat.' (v.5, TLB)

The only person who filled Elijah's vision was Jehovah, but now he looks through the wrong end of the telescope, and his perspective is greatly distorted. Once we take our eyes off God, then despair and disillusionment soon set in. Elijah becomes deeply depressed, and prays that God might take away his life. Instead, God lovingly encourages him to eat, sleep and relax. How easy it is in spiritual service to neglect physical and emotional needs. Beware of the trap into which Elijah fell, and make sure, however spiritually motivated you are, that you have time to relax, unwind and take care of your physical and emotional needs.

Father, help me to be a balanced Christian, one who neither burns out nor rusts out, but lives out Your purposes here on earth. Amen.

LIVING OUT GOD'S MESSAGE

FOR READING AND MEDITATION
Hosea 1:1–3

*'The Lord said to Hosea, "Go and marry ...
a prostitute ... This will illustrate the way my
people have been untrue to me ..."' (v.2, TLB)*

Why would God lead one of his prophets into such a
difficult marriage? In Exodus 24:3, Israel entered
into a covenant with the Lord, that they would be faithful
to Him. This was similar to a marriage vow but now
the nation, by flirting with other gods, was guilty of
unfaithfulness and adultery. In effect, God says to Hosea,
'I need your help. I have marriage problems, too. Stick to
Gomer, no matter what happens, and perhaps the nation
will comprehend through your actions something of my
undying love.' Hosea faced an astonishing request from
God – not only to preach His message, but live it.

**Father, help me not just to preach to others with words,
but to live out Your message of love for Your people.
Amen.**

GOD'S PLAN UNFOLDS

FOR READING AND MEDITATION
Hosea 1:4–11

'… *Call her Lo-Ruhamah, for I will no longer show love … Call him Lo-Ammi, for you are not my people …' (vv.6,9)*

osea was entitled to have his wife thrown into a pit and be stoned to death. However, he chose to forgive. His love was too strong to be broken by Gomer's infidelities, and he was obliged to consider God's interest in his marriage, too. After all, his marriage was to be a 'visual aid' for Israel so that they could see what was happening in the bigger 'marriage' between themselves and the Almighty. The marriage breakdown was part of God's plan. The Almighty wanted to show Israel that if she kept flirting with other gods, she, too, would be discarded and disowned. This grim warning is reflected in the names Hosea gave to his wife's three children.

Father, help me to have the patience and forgiving love of Your servant Hosea. For Jesus' sake. Amen.

LOVE NEVER FAILS

Hosea 2:1–14

*'But I will court her again, and bring her into the
wilderness, and speak to her tenderly there.'
(v.14, TLB)*

Hosea's marriage and family was an object lesson to
Israel. Gomer's unfaithfulness symbolised Israel's
impurity and corruption, and the names of the children
reflected God's revulsion at the spiritual and moral
condition of Israel. As Hosea waited before God he came to
see that his own situation, though painful and depressing,
was as nothing compared to the hurt in God's heart. His
own heartbreak was measured in months and years, but
God's torment over Israel spanned the centuries. Soon,
however, the waiting must end. Hosea would win back
Gomer just as God would win back His people in Israel.
True love never fails.

**Father, help me in my own relationships to be
convinced of the fact that love never fails and help me
keep on loving. Amen.**

BIBLE BIOGRAPHIES

A TIME OF RECKONING

FOR READING AND MEDITATION

Hosea 3:1–5

- - - - - - - - - - - - - - - - - -

'The LORD said to me, "Go, show your love to your wife again ..."' (v.1)

When Hosea arrives home with his wife, he explains that for a while there was to be no physical relationship. To Gomer, love was merely a matter of sex. This is what she had lived for. However, now she must learn what love and marriage are all about. God's bride must learn a similar lesson too, says Hosea: '... Israel will be a long time without a king or prince, and without an altar, temple, priests, or even idols!' (v.4, TLB). Like Gomer, Israel was taken up with the physical side of her relationship with God – leaders, sacrifices, rituals and ceremonies. She used religious objects as Gomer had used sex. Now comes a time of reckoning.

Father, help me not to do as Israel did – become preoccupied with physical things and withhold my heart from You. Amen.

BREACH OF PROMISE

Hosea 4:1–19

'Hear the word of the Lord, O people of Israel.
The Lord has filed a lawsuit against you ...'
(v.1, TLB)

Hosea started to view Israel from God's standpoint. God shows him that He has 'filed a lawsuit' against Israel, and that Hosea is to be His spokesman and advocate (v.1). Israel had refused to accept God as her one true husband. She had violated her marriage vows and flirted with other gods. This problem now ends up in the high court of heaven, and charges are levelled against the unfaithful bride. The charge is breach of promise. Hosea, as God's representative, has the task of informing Israel of her sentence, and much of what follows in this book is God's indictment of His people. They are about to find out that independence and sin do not pay.

Father, You are not blind to sin in the life of those You love – and it is a love that disciplines to improve. Amen.

GOD YEARNS FOR OUR LOVE

Hosea 5:1–6:1

'Listen to this, you priests and all of Israel's leaders ...' (5:1, TLB)

Hosea takes the message to the priests and leaders of the nation. Hosea was the right man to tell Israel about God's loving concern, for having suffered himself, he could identify both with the message and with God. Hosea loved Gomer so much that he was prepared to suffer separation if in the long run it would teach her the importance of faithfulness. Israel would be turned out of her homeland, her altars torn down and her temples smashed. Israel had offered cows and sheep as a device to keep God happy while they pursued their own selfish interests. They failed to hear the Almighty's plaintive cry: 'I want your love; I don't want your offerings' (6:6, TLB).

Father, help me to see that rebellion is hurtful to You, not simply because it breaks Your laws, but because it wounds Your heart. Amen.

GENUINE LOVE IS SUFFERING LOVE

FOR READING AND MEDITATION

Hosea 14:1–9

'... *my love will know no bounds, for my anger will be forever gone!*' (v.4, TLB)

What a compelling picture of God Hosea gives in this last chapter. Even though His heart is broken, He plans for the good of His people and for their reconciliation to Him. And why? Hosea takes us to the answer in chapter 11, verse 9, 'For I am God, and not man.' His love is eternal, boundless and incomprehensible. The life of Hosea can be summarised by saying that here is a man who not only spoke God's message but lived it. Such was his strength of character that God was able to use him as an object lesson to the whole of Israel, showing them what suffering love was all about.

Father, bring me closer I pray to Your purposes for my life and keep me from following false gods. In Jesus' name. Amen.

THE MAN WHO SAID 'NO'

Jonah 1:1–3

'But Jonah was afraid to go and ran away from the Lord.' (v.3, TLB)

G od had told His people how to differentiate between
a true prophet and a false prophet: 'If what a prophet
proclaims in the name of the LORD does not take place
or come true, that is a message the LORD has not spoken'
(Deut. 18:22). Jonah ponders the fact that if he prophesies
against Nineveh, and the people repent then God will
change His mind and suspend His judgment, which might
cause some to say, 'Jonah is a prophet who cannot tell what
is going to happen.' His concern for his own reputation
caused him to put his own interest before God's. And that
is one of life's greatest absurdities.

**Father, may Your interest be more important than
my interests. Help me to side with You against myself.
Amen.**

'HE PAID THE FARE'

Jonah 1:1–7

'… so he paid the fare, and went on board …'
(v.3, RSV)

Jonah paid heavily to run away from God – and so
do we. God is our life, and when we run away from
Him we run away from all that makes us whole. We then
learn the hard way – as Jonah did. We pay the price in
inner conflicts and guilt – things which, in themselves,
become our own punishment. Jonah represents a study of
an escape mentality. He thought that on his own he would
be free but that under God he would be in bondage. He
was free – free to get himself into trouble and free to go
from entanglement to entanglement. 'He paid the fare' of
disobedience.

**Father, to play truant with You is to play truant with
myself, and I will pay for the consequences. Help me be
obedient. Amen.**

PENANCE – NOT REPENTANCE

FOR READING AND MEDITATION

Jonah 1:1–17

- - - - - - - - - - - - - - - - - - - -

'... the Lord flung a terrific wind over the sea, causing a great storm ...' (v.4, TLB)

Anyone who runs away from God is heading for a storm. It may not happen on the outside, but it will certainly happen within. Fears, worries, conflicts, guilt, all combine to form a boiling tempest in the heart of the person trying to get away from God. Jonah's request to be thrown into the sea was another form of escapism and self-punishment. But penance is not repentance. Penance tries to make atonement for its sin by its own suffering; repentance is sorrow for one's sin, and a turning to God for cleansing and renewal. All other ways of escape are futile.

Father, help me to take Your way of full confession and repentance and not any other way – for Your way always works. Amen.

A SECOND CHANCE

Jonah 2:1–10

'From inside the fish Jonah prayed to the LORD his God.' (v.1)

Jonah was willing to go overboard but not willing to go to Nineveh – willing to do everything except the right thing. So God had to let him soak in some digestive juices for a few days to soften him up! In the belly of the great fish, Jonah resolves that if God brings him out of the situation alive, he will sing 'a song of thanksgiving' and offer God a sacrifice. When it comes to the failures of his servants, God is the God of the second chance. And so, once again, it is time for God to act. He orders the fish 'to spit up Jonah on the beach, and it did' (v.10, TLB).

Father, despite my stubbornness or wilfulness when I fail to fulfil Your purposes, You are the God of the second chance. Thank You, Lord. Amen.

THE INNER REBEL

Jonah 3:1–10

'Then the word of the LORD came to Jonah a second time ...' (v.1)

God comes to Jonah a second time with instructions to go to Nineveh, and call on its inhabitants to repent. The man who said 'No' becomes the man who said 'Yes'. But how committed was Jonah to fulfilling God's purposes? Was his heart now really in the task? I think not. He was Jonah still – the inward runaway. He went and yet he didn't. He was outwardly conforming but inwardly rebelling. Although everyone in Nineveh repented and was happy they had been spared God's judgment, this could not be said of Jonah. 'The change of plans,' say the Scriptures, 'made Jonah very angry' (4:1, TLB).

Father, may I not just outwardly obey You, but may I inwardly delight to do Your will and happily accept Your judgments. Amen.

'NOW LOOK WHAT YOU MADE ME DO'

Jonah 4:1–3

'... I'd rather be dead than alive (when nothing that I told them happens).' (v.3, TLB)

Jonah's response to God's change of mind is a desire to die. He blames God for his feelings. He is still trying to run away, to escape. Since Jonah had not given up his basic attitudes he manifests them in this crisis. Whenever he gets into a major difficulty he wants to die. He is not only still running away, he is still punishing himself, or proposing to do so by asking that God takes his life. Whenever there is incomplete repentance then guilt remains, creating an unstable personality which jumps from subterfuge to subterfuge to get temporary relief from an inner ache – the ache of basic disobedience.

Father, help me to be a stable person with all my guilt forgiven and inner conflicts resolved through the power of the cross. Amen.

THE MAN WHO MIGHT HAVE BEEN

Jonah 4:4–11

'So Jonah went out and sat sulking …' (v.5, TLB)

As Jonah sits sulking, he cares only for himself and not for the people. He was more interested in vindicating himself than in the salvation of a people who were under the judgment of God. It is quite obvious that Jonah had an unsurrendered ego. God exposes Jonah's self-centredness because he is more interested in his own comfortable shade than the death of thousands. Jonah is still running away – from himself and the caring person he could have been. He could have gone down in history as the prophet who, under God, brought about the salvation of a great city. Instead he goes down as a man who kept running – running from both God and himself.

O God, save me from running away from You and the person You have called me to be. May compassion, not comfort, motivate me. Amen.

FROM CONFUSION TO CONFIDENCE

FOR READING AND MEDITATION

Habakkuk 1:1–4

*'Must I forever see this sin and sadness
all around me?' (v.3, TLB)*

Habakkuk was confused and frustrated by the continuance of evil. He could not understand why God did not intervene to restrain the evil nations around him. Some regard his direct questioning of God as impertinent, but God doesn't fall off His throne when one of His children asks Him a direct and searching question. God can take it! Habakkuk did what everyone should do when they cannot understand the ways of the Almighty – talk to God about it. Don't expect to win any argument with God, but be assured that when you pour out your anxieties and frustrations, He will most certainly listen. The most important thing anyone can do when they are confused is to admit it.

Father, help me to admit to confusion and not repress it, so I can move into a new confidence. In Jesus' name. Amen.

THE PAIN OF ANSWERED PRAYER

Habakkuk 1:5–11

- -

'You will be astounded at what I am about to do!' (v.5, TLB)

Will God answer the prophet in his confusion? He does, but not in the way Habakkuk anticipated. The Almighty announces that he is about to use an evil and cruel nation, the Chaldeans, to prune and purify His people. We sometimes hear Christians talk of the pain of unanswered prayer. 'What can be more painful,' they say, 'than the pain of unanswered prayer?' I will tell you – the pain of answered prayer. The answer our prayers receive is not always the answer our hearts desire. He who asks God for light must not complain if at times the light scorches. God is too loving to deny us the truth.

Father, the answers I get are not always the ones I want. Help me at such times to bear the pain of answered prayer. Amen.

ESTABLISHING PERSPECTIVE

Habakkuk 1:12–17

'O LORD, are you not from everlasting?
My God, my Holy One ...' (v.12)

Habakkuk establishes a spiritual context and perspective for his problem by focusing on God's character. The art of navigation depends on the existence of certain fixed points – a star, a headland, a rock. No one can take a bearing from a cloud, because a cloud is not fixed. On the voyage of life we must have fixed points. And what are those fixed points? The life of our Lord is a fixed point. The cross is a fixed point. The love of God is a fixed point. Let's learn to navigate by these fixed points, and take our bearing from the things we know, rather than the things we do not know.

Father, I will never understand what You do unless I understand more about who You are. Help me know You more. Amen.

LIVING BY FAITH

FOR READING AND MEDITATION

Habakkuk 2:1–5

'… the righteous will live by his faith …' (v.4)

O ne of the hardest things to do in life is to sit back and wait for God to fulfil His purposes. To learn that God has a perfect timing for His purposes, and to outgrow the impatience which demands an answer immediately and on our terms, is one of life's greatest victories. As Habakkuk waited before God he received a revelation – 'the righteous will live by his faith'. In a sense Habakkuk's confusion can be summarised in these words: how can a man keep his faith? Here then is God's answer: his faith shall keep him. We do not understand God, but we do trust God.

Father, I realise now that I want to see before I believe. But help me to believe even though I cannot see. Amen.

GOD – THE RULER OF HISTORY

Habakkuk 2:6–20

'For the earth will be filled with the knowledge of the glory of the LORD, as the waters cover the sea.' (v.14)

Habakkuk was confused when he learned that God was going to use the Babylonian armies to prune His own people, but God used their plans to carry out His. Eventually God would judge the Babylonians also. God is the ruler of history so Habakkuk eventually got God's point that history is 'His-story'. God knows what He is doing even when history seems to be speeding downhill like a car out of control. And the same word that brought comfort to Habakkuk can, if we let it, comfort our hearts. In this nuclear age, just as in Bible days, the eternal God is in complete control and will reign gloriously.

Father, what relief it brings me, to recognise that You are the Lord of history and the One who is in final control. Hallelujah!

GOD CAN DO IT AGAIN

Habakkuk 3:1–15

'... I stand in awe of your deeds, O LORD.
Renew them in our day, in our time make
them known ...' (v.2)

The way in which God led Habakkuk from confusion
to confidence can be seen from the matchless words of
this third chapter. The chapter begins with prayer and ends
with praise. Despite the fact that Habakkuk's confidence
in God has grown and developed, he still feels the need to
pray for a spiritual revival: 'O LORD, revive your work in
the midst of the years' (v.2, NKJV). No matter how dark
the situation, and no matter how gloomy the outlook,
it is always right to seek God for a Holy Spirit revival.
Make this a special plea to God today, I beg you: 'You did it
before, Lord – now do it again.'

**Lord, everything within me cries out for a spiritual
awakening in this day and age. You did it before –
now do it again. Amen.**

HINDS' FEET ON HIGH PLACES

Habakkuk 3:16–19

'... he makes my feet like hinds' feet, he makes me tread upon ... high places.' (v.19, RSV)

Habakkuk no longer stumbles along in the midst of darkness and doubt, but leaps from one revelation to another with the steady, surefootedness of a deer. He walks safely upon high places where others are afraid to tread. By climbing his watchtower to enter into a dialogue with God, Habakkuk has learned so much that his soul is lifted above the doubts and uncertainties that once plagued his mind. The prophet began in confusion, as we *often* do – and ended in confidence, as we *can* do. What made the difference? He saw that God was Lord and would trust Him even if harvests failed and food was scarce. It is as simple as that!

Father, You rule in all things, and when I spend time with You I can move from confusion to confidence. Amen.

ONLY THE BEST IS GOOD ENOUGH

FOR READING AND MEDITATION
Malachi 1:1–14

'Cursed is the cheat who has an acceptable male in his flock ... but then sacrifices a blemished animal to the Lord.' (v.14)

The people had begun to take God for granted and had lost their sense of spiritual need. Even their sacrifices were inadequate. Today, of course, animal sacrifices are unnecessary as Christ's death has made a full atonement for our sin. We are still obliged, however, to honour God as Father and Master. If we fail to honour Him as God and neglect to give Him His due – time, money, energy, concern – then this is the moment when we ought to re-establish our priorities. A man who offered an unfit sacrifice in Old Testament times was called a cheat. We, too, fall into this category when we refuse to give Him our best.

Father, help me to establish You as my number one priority and always give You my best. For Jesus' sake. Amen.

VOTING GOD'S WAY

Malachi 2:1–9

'Priests' lips should flow with the knowledge of God so the people will learn God's laws.' (v.7, TLB)

Malachi criticised the priests for failing to teach the people accurately and faithfully all aspects of the divine law. We can have good music and entertaining services, but if there is no sound biblical teaching then they are an empty pantomime. What is happening to the teaching ministry in today's Church? Do our young people grasp the full meaning and implication of the Christian faith? Are we showing them how to live by the values revealed in the Bible? Do we give them clear biblical instruction on how to cope with sexual permissiveness, problems of authority and matters of morality? We should become less concerned about voting man's way and more concerned about voting God's way.

Father, create in us a deeper hunger for Your Word, and raise up faithful teachers who will present it without fear or compromise. Amen.

'HATE DIVORCE'

Malachi 2:10–16

'... the Lord has seen your treachery in divorcing your wives who have been faithful to you through the years ...' (v.14, TLB)

I am convinced that if we saw divorce as God sees it, we would approach marriage problems with a good deal more determination to resolve them than we do at present. Human nature is such that when romance begins to fade in a marriage it becomes so easy to simply divorce. In an age when there is an increasing acceptance of divorce as the only solution to marital problems, let those of us who are the Lord's children resist this pressure with all the energy we can. Instead, let us choose to resolve our marital problems by reference to the Word of God, the power of the Spirit of God and help from the people of God.

O Father, send the reinforcing breath of the Spirit through every Christian marriage to renew and strengthen them. For Jesus' sake. Amen.

SERVING GOD WITH MAMMON

Malachi 2:17–3:15

'Will a man rob God? Yet you rob me.' (3:8)

We can rob God by not tithing but we can also rob God by only tithing and thinking the rest is ours to do with as we like. Ultimately, everything belongs to God. A tithe actually recognises God's ownership of all our possessions, just as we pay rent to acknowledge the ownership of the landlord over our home. When you relinquish ownership of your possessions to God, life takes on a sense of stewardship. You are handling something on behalf of Another. That does something to the whole of life – puts sacredness into the secular. Money becomes a message. You cannot serve God *and* Mammon, but you can serve God *with* Mammon.

Father, I live in an acquisitive society where worth is judged by wealth. Help me to acknowledge You are the true owner of everything. Amen.

GET BACK TO THE BIBLE

Malachi 3:16–4:6

'But for you who fear my name, the Sun of Righteousness will rise with healing in his wings.'
(4:2, TLB)

Malachi underlines the importance of living in obedience to God's commands and principles. There were those in his day (as in ours) who attempted to achieve happiness and success by ignoring the moral laws which God has built into the universe. But such a way was a way of failure and discontent. What is involved in living responsibly in an age when moral issues are somewhat vague and indistinct? It means developing a set of values based on God's Word and deliberately sticking to them, even when it is hard to do so. The time has come for 21st-century Christians to have their vision refocused – and that can happen only when we get back to the Bible.

Father, thank You for the example of people from the Old Testament. May their faith inspire me and may I in turn inspire others. Amen.

NOVEMBER 1
GOD'S CONCERNS

FOR READING AND MEDITATION
1 John 4:7–21

*'Dear friends, since God loved as much as that,
we surely ought to love each other too.' (v.11, TLB)*

What is life's greatest purpose? This: *to be aware of
God, and aware of others.* You may already be aware
of God but how aware are you of others? Do you know
about their problems and, if so, do you actually care about
them? Have you a genuine concern for people in trouble?
Someone said: 'Most human problems stem from the fact
that we treat people as things and things as people.' God's
highest priority in the universe is to do with people. He
created them and when He saw their needs He shed His
own blood for them. If we are to discover God's purpose
for our lives then we must bring our concerns in line with
His concerns.

**Father, help me to more fully understand Your concerns
and make them my concerns. For Jesus' sake. Amen.**

A UNIVERSAL CRAVING

Philippians 3:1–14

'… I keep going on, trying to grasp that purpose for which Christ Jesus grasped me.' (v.12, Phillips)

Every system of philosophy, whether religious or not, is really a human attempt to satisfy the craving in our lives to be pointed in the right direction. A Christian need not be in any doubt about the direction in which God wants him to go and what is the Creator's highest purpose for his life. It is receiving God's love, and then channelling that love into the lives of those around us who are weak and wounded. God wants you to be a caring person, sensitive to the needs of others and aware of the way in which He wants you to minister to them. Once you grasp this then you are on your way to fulfilling your highest destiny.

Father, I am on this earth for a high and noble purpose. Make that purpose more clear to me day by day. Amen.

A CHRISTIAN — ONE WHO CARES

FOR READING AND MEDITATION
1 Corinthians 12:12–26

'... that the members may have the same care for one another.' (v.25, RSV)

Baron Von Huegel, a Roman Catholic layman, once gave this penetrating definition of a Christian: 'A Christian is one who cares.' How caring are you? Today you might rub shoulders with someone who is ready to come apart at the seams – but unless you are deeply sensitive, you might never notice it. All around us people are crying out to be loved, but many of us pursue our own desires with little or no understanding of the marvellous purpose that God has for us – to lift the fallen, cheer the fainthearted and give hope to the hopeless. We are so wrapped up in our own purposes that we miss His purposes.

Father, help me embrace Your purposes for, by doing so, I know I shall be walking with destiny. Amen.

A GOD WHO CARES

Romans 5:1–11

'When we were utterly helpless, with no way of escape, Christ came at just the right time and died for us sinners who had no use for him.' (v.6, TLB)

A Hindu doctor said, 'We must not involve God in the affairs of this world. He is lifted above all these things. We must not humanise God.' In other words, God to him was a God who didn't care. But a God who doesn't care, doesn't count. The God who would sit in awful isolation, separated from the problems and difficulties of His creation, is not worth considering. However, God has, by His own volition, entered through the door of humanity and involved Himself with us in the Person of His Son, Jesus Christ. No other god can speak to my condition for no other god was in my condition. Our God is a God who cares.

Father, I see so clearly that You are a God who cares – really cares. And because You care, I must care too. Amen.

THE LAW OF CHRIST

Mark 10:46–52

- -

'When Jesus heard him he stopped there in the road and said, "Tell him to come here."' (v.49, TLB)

Before Jesus noticed him, the people had little or no interest in the blind man. Their response to his plea for Jesus to help him was: 'Shut up!' When, however, Jesus said, 'Tell him to come here,' they rushed over to him and said, 'Come on, he's calling you!' Now Jesus' interest became their interest. Something similar must happen to us. Although by nature we might not be caring people, we must live in such a close relationship with Jesus Christ that His concerns become our concerns, His sensitivity becomes our sensitivity, His interests become our interests. In Galatians 6:2, the 'law of Christ' is the law of caring by sharing others' burdens.

O God, help me to live by the law of Christ – the law of caring by sharing the burdens of others. Amen.

THE SECOND INCARNATION

John 20:19–31

'As the Father has sent me, even so I send you.'
(v.21, RSV)

The New Testament teaches that today Christ can be seen and found in the words and loving deeds of His disciples – you and me. Someone has daringly called this extension of Christ's care and compassion, as expressed through the lives of His followers, 'the second incarnation'. Just as in the first incarnation God came in the Person of His Son, Jesus Christ, to show humanity that He cared, so in the second incarnation (His divine indwelling in His Church), He is present in the world to spell out that same wondrous message – God cares. A YMCA official said in the organisation's early days: 'We see a need, we pray about it and we do something about it.'

Father, we can be good at seeing needs and praying about needs but help us also to do something about needs. Amen.

LIFE IS SENSITIVITY

Matthew 25:31–46

'For I was hungry and you gave me something to eat ... I was in prison and you came to visit me. (vv.35–36)

One man defined life as 'sensitivity'. This is an interesting definition, for when we examine life in all its aspects, we find that the lowest form of life is sensitive only to itself. He went on to say, 'You can tell how high you have risen in the scale of life by asking yourself the question: How widely and how deeply do I care? When you rise to the highest level of life ever demonstrated on this earth – the life of Jesus – you find total sensitivity. Jesus said on one occasion, 'Whatever you did for one of the least brothers of mine, you did for me.' He was hungry in their hunger, bound in their imprisonment.

Father, I need a baptism of caring love to flow in and through my personality so that I can truly be sensitive to others. Amen.

OUR MAJOR CONCERN

FOR READING AND MEDITATION
Galatians 6:1–10

'... *we should always be kind to everyone, and especially to our Christian brothers.*' (v.10, TLB)

While we must have a genuine concern for everyone, our major concern must be towards our fellow Christians. If the Church was healthy and mainly filled with mature Christians, then we would not need to be involved in so much aggressive evangelism. The non-Christian, seeing a joyous and loving Church, would be drawn towards it by the sheer attractiveness of love. Lack of spiritual maturity in believers is a deterrent to others receiving the gospel. We must get things the right way round, and thus avoid the criticism made by many that the Church is the only society that doesn't take care of its wounded.

O Father, I commit myself today to this task of helping fellow Christians so the Church becomes strong and attractive. Amen.

THE MAIN FOCUS

1 Peter 4:12–19

'For it is time for judgment to begin with the family of God ...' (v.17)

I am not against evangelism. I have been an evangelist for most of my Christian life. But the Church generally is weak and seriously lacking in love, joy and maturity. How can we say we care for sinners if we don't care for those who are part of the family of God? Jesus did not say, 'By this all men will know that you are my disciples, if you hold evangelistic rallies in big stadiums.' No, He said, ' By this all men will know that you are my disciples, if you love one another' (John 13:35). The world listens when Christians love.

O Father, You cut through our lives with the sword of Your Spirit to prune us to love and be more like Jesus. Amen.

CANNIBAL CHRISTIANS

Galatians 5:13–26

'If you keep on biting and devouring each other, watch out or you will be destroyed by each other.' (v.15)

Although there are many churches where love and care are practised by the members towards each other, there are far too many where it is not. In fact, many are nests of hate, where instead of love and care, there exists spite and spleen. Are there any 'cannibal Christians' in your church? If the sheep are not protected from the wolves, then it is to be expected that they will get bitten, but no shepherd would expect his sheep to get bitten in the barn! The tragedy in some of our churches is that often the greatest wounds come not from the wolves but from other sheep.

O Father, send the wind of Your caring love through every part of Your Church. For Jesus' sake. Amen.

ETHOS, PATHOS AND LOGIA

1 Corinthians 13:1–13

'If I ... have not love, I am nothing.' (v.2)

Aristotle said that a messenger had to have three things – ethos, pathos and logia. First, he must have ethos, which is related to our word 'ethical' and refers to integrity. The second quality is pathos, which means sympathy or empathy. The third quality is logia, closely related to 'logos' or 'word' – the one who communicates must have something worthwhile to say. The Greeks recognised that oratorical skill without a caring heart added up to nothing. 'Eloquence without love,' said the apostle, 'is a sounding brass and a tinkling cymbal.' An American evangelist, Floyd McClung, put it succinctly when he said, 'People don't care how much we know until they know how much we care.'

Father, save us from becoming self-centred and uncaring so our message is lost because of lack of feeling for our hearers. Amen.

STEREOPHONIC SAINTS

FOR READING AND MEDITATION

1 Peter 3:8–22

- -

'Quietly trust yourself to Christ your Lord and if anybody asks why you believe as you do, be ready to tell him, and do it in a gentle and respectful way.'
(v.15, TLB)

Songs are made up of lyrics and music. Lyrics, without musical accompaniment, lose much of their impact. We must be ready to tell our message (words) but in a gentle and respectful way (music). Evangelism is to be stereophonic. God speaks to His erring creatures through two channels: the written Word (the Bible) and you – His 'living epistle'. The best argument for Christianity is Christians – their joy, their love, their care and concern. The Church of today has the best lyrics but some very poor music. Let's begin to play the music of caring love, and then the world will be more ready to listen to the Word.

Father, help us – Your people – to be truly stereophonic, sharing the love of Jesus both by our lips and by our lives. Amen.

THE MUSIC OF THE GOSPEL

Matthew 5:1–16

'... that they may see your good deeds and praise your Father in heaven.' (v.16)

Christians are to *be* good news before they *share* the good news. Evangelism would be far more effective if the music of the gospel preceded the words and thus prepared the hearts of the people for what is to follow. As the gospel makes an impact on a person's life, and works its way out through their relationships so that their lifestyle is transformed, then that becomes the music. When the world observes Christian couples loving each other, and both husbands and wives supporting and caring for their families, when they see churches overflowing with care and concern, they have seen a miracle – they have heard the music.

Father, help me to be such a loving, caring person that even though I may stumble over my lines, the music will play on. Amen.

OUT OF BUSINESS

Revelation 2:1–7

'If you do not repent, I will come to you and remove your lampstand from its place.' (v.5)

The theologically orthodox Church at Ephesus was warned by God that if she did not recover her love, then He would remove her candlestick – put her out of business. God is saying the same thing to the churches of this generation: 'Demonstrate love, or I will withdraw My presence.' Can it be that many of the places where people meet on Sundays to sing a few hymns are churches in name only? Honesty compels us to admit that this may be so. If a church does not focus on conducting God's business – being a loving, caring community – then it must not complain if, in due course, it finds itself out of business!

Lord, You shared Your love with me, not just in words but with a fire in my soul. May I spark the same fire in others. Amen.

SELF-CENTRED – SELF-DISRUPTED

Romans 15:1–13

'We who are strong ought to bear with the failings of the weak and not to please ourselves.' (v.1)

What happens if we fail to reach out and help others? The answer is that we become inextricably involved with ourselves and our own problems and troubles. It can be said that every self-centred person is an unhappy person – no exceptions. This matter of centring on oneself works badly – in fact, it works havoc on the very self which is being centred upon. Every self-centred person is a disrupted person, and the disruption doesn't merely stop with the soul or the spirit; it extends straight out into the nerves and tissues, and poisons them with functional and structural disease. More people are being broken by self-centredness than any other one single thing in life.

Father, release me from self-centredness and into Christ-centredness, so my thoughts and concerns are about others. In Jesus' name. Amen.

TO SAVE – IS TO LOSE

Mark 8:31–38

'For whoever wants to save his life
will lose it ...' (v.35)

More people are broken by self-centredness than any other one thing in life. The text before us today: 'For whoever wants to save his life will lose it ...' underlines the fact that when we concentrate on ourselves, the self will go to pieces. A doctor said, 'That is the end of egocentrics. They start out to draw life to themselves – its joys, its thrills – and all they succeed in drawing to themselves is sadness, loneliness, disillusionment and sickness – spiritual, mental and physical.' When we concentrate on ourselves alone, then the law of the universe goes into operation – we save our life only to lose it.

Father, help me to go with Your laws rather than go against them. Help me to live for others – then I will truly live. Amen.

PEOPLE – PICKLED IN THEMSELVES

Romans 14:1–13

'For none of us lives to himself alone ...' (v.7)

We continue examining a very important principle of life – that when we follow a policy of reaching out to others and caring for them, we become less and less concerned about our own troubles and difficulties, and less and less prone to personality problems. The mental health specialists are beginning to emphasise what the Bible has been emphasising for centuries, that to save one's life, one has to give it. Some forms of mental illness are generated by physical factors, I know. Many people, however, are tied up inwardly and are 'walking conflicts'. They stay in normal relationships only to make them abnormal by their inner conflicts.

Father, please release me completely from the claims of self-interest and self-centredness. In Christ's name I pray. Amen.

THE PURPOSE OF THE ATONEMENT

2 Corinthians 5:11–21

'... he died for all in order to have the living live no longer for themselves ...' (v.15, Moffatt)

We are quietly coming to the conclusion that we were created by God to be caring and concerned people and when we abandon this divine design for one of self-interest we live against life's great purpose and end up with inner conflicts and self-disruption. Our text for today spells out the good news that one of the chief ends of Christ's atonement is to deliver us from self-centred preoccupation. Have you experienced the freeing power of the cross in relation to this matter of your self-centeredness? Some experience it in a dramatic moment of conversion. Most, however, find it some time after conversion in a period of enlightenment and challenge, such as our current study.

Father, I am so thankful that Your atonement did not pass by my central need – the need of deliverance from myself. Amen.

NOVEMBER 19
SELF-SURRENDER

FOR READING AND MEDITATION
Galatians 3:1–14

'After beginning with the Spirit, are you now trying to attain your goal by human effort?' (v.3)

The three most popular views of the self are: know yourself, accept yourself and express yourself. All three are valid concepts, providing they are linked with Christ and not divorced from Him. You are a child of God, made in His likeness, and so it follows that you can only know yourself as you know Him. Also, it is only when a person has been changed by Christ that he is truly able to accept himself. Outside of Christ, what kind of self can a person express? Only an egocentric self, a proud self, a sinful self. The secular way of putting self in the centre lacks the vital principle which only the Christian faith offers – surrender of self.

Father, I realise I am on the verge of discovering one of life's greatest secrets – deliverance from self by self-surrender. Amen.

DISCOVERING LIFE'S GREATEST PURPOSE

A WILLING CRUCIFIXION

FOR READING AND MEDITATION

Galatians 2:11–21

'I have been crucified with Christ and I no longer live, but Christ lives in me.' (v.20)

The principle of self-surrender is this – the self, or ego, is offered up lovingly, as Jesus offered Himself up on the cross. Christ's offering was done out of love – our offering of our self to be crucified with Him must also be out of love. We love Him so much that we can withhold nothing from Him – not even our very self. When we willingly consent to be crucified with Christ, we die with Him and rise with Him. No longer do we live for ourselves, but for Him. After the self-surrender of being crucified with Christ, Paul was more alive than ever: 'Christ lives in me.' Christ, who is life, was living in him – and how!

Father, I willingly offer myself to You: that self might die and Christ might live in me, heightening all my powers. Amen.

GAZING AT SUFFERING LOVE

Philippians 2:1–11

'Your attitude should be the same as that of Christ Jesus ...' (v.5)

A teenager was told that if she stayed out late she would get bread and water for supper. She did, and at supper time she was given bread and water. After a few minutes the father reached over and took the bread and water giving his daughter his own meal instead. Something broke inside her. Self-will was broken and 'father-will' gently substituted by her own choice. No threat of punishment, no fear of consequence could work that miracle. Only suffering love could do that. So stand before the cross and gaze upward into that loving face. See how suffering love has taken your punishment and pain and walk away from the cross, free from self-interest and self-concern.

Lord, I accept Your full and complete deliverance from self. Delivered from myself, I am now free to give myself to others. Amen.

DISCOVERING LIFE'S GREATEST PURPOSE

CARING IS COMMITMENT

James 4:7–17

- - - - - - - - - - - - - - - - - - -

'Anyone, then, who knows the good he ought to do and doesn't do it, sins.' (v.17)

Christian caring is attending to the welfare of another person in ways that help the person see and understand the character of Christ as manifested through our deeds, our words and our actions. Caring is more than liking a person, comforting a person or showing sympathy to a person. Caring is a commitment: an action of the will which is dedicated to obeying another deep law of the universe – it is more blessed to give than to receive. It is important to recognise that caring is more than a feeling, mood or emotion: it is an attitude of mind that applies itself to doing what God expects of us whether we feel like it or not.

O God, help me not to be guided by my feelings but by a dedicated will. In Jesus' name I pray. Amen.

CARING IS LISTENING

FOR READING AND MEDITATION

James 1:19–27

'… *it is best to listen much …*' (*v.19, TLB*)

What does caring mean in real and practical terms?
Caring involves listening. One of the most caring
things we can do for people is to listen to them. Listening
is an art. It begins with the way we use our eyes. If you
look beyond a person instead of at them, the message they
receive is that you are not all that deeply interested in what
they are saying. Dr Julias Fast says, 'If you hold another
person's eye longer than say two seconds, it's a clear sign
to them that you are interested in what they are saying.'
Now don't overdo this and stare into people's eyes, but do
develop your listening skills.

**Father, You never turn away from me, but always listen.
If caring means listening, then make me a good listener.
For Jesus' sake. Amen.**

CARING IS TOUCHING

FOR READING AND MEDITATION
Matthew 8:1–4

'Jesus reached out his hand and touched the man.' (v.3)

Caring often involves touching. During the nineteenth century a high percentage of infants in orphanages died from a disease called marasmus. A Dr Chapin noted that infants were rarely picked up or touched, so he brought in women to hold the babies, coo to them and stroke them. The mortality rate dropped drastically. If you want to demonstrate to others that you care, be aware of the power of touch. But here again, don't overdo it. When someone is hurting, reach out to them, put a hand gently on theirs or touch them gently on the shoulder. When done as a genuine attempt to show you care, it can bring you closer to a person than a thousand words.

Lord, make me a person with a tender touch, and show me how to use, and not abuse, this means of communication. Amen.

CARING IS EMPATHY

2 Corinthians 1:1–11

'... who comforts us in all our troubles, so that we can comfort those in any trouble ...' (v.4)

Sympathy is subjective: it gets down into the pit with a person and shares his feelings of hurt. Empathy is objective: it seeks to understand the hurt, without going down into the pit, so that it can lift the other person to safety and security. This is why I prefer to use the word 'empathy'– it is a more objective and more appropriate word in the present context. We can all develop a level of empathy. It involves a continuous, active effort to understand what is going on inside the other person's heart. Ask yourself questions like this: How would I feel if I were in this person's circumstances? How would I react if this had happened to me?

Father, help me to become a truly empathic person – one who can feel for others without being swamped by those feelings. Amen.

CARING IS RESPECT

FOR READING AND MEDITATION
Romans 12:9–21

'… give each other priority out of respect for one another.' (v.10, Translator's)

Caring is showing respect. A research project was conducted among a group of well-known psychiatrists and counsellors to discover what qualities made them successful. The common denominator was that they treated their clients with respect. Unless we are careful, whenever we are confronted by individuals in need, we can adopt the attitude, 'Isn't it wonderful that I am going to help you!' or 'How on earth did you allow yourself to get into such a mess? I would never have done such a thing.' Good caring avoids such attitudes. Respect means that we care for people too much to judge them, categorise them, label them or manipulate them. Remember, Jesus was called 'the friend of sinners'.

Father, remove from my heart any wrong attitudes that may be there, and help me to relate to people with love, care and respect. Amen.

CARING IS HOPE

Matthew 7:7–12

'Ask and it will be given to you ...' (v.7)

Caring is giving hope. There is a natural hope based on human reasoning and optimism. The hope that I am referring to, however, is a Christian hope: the hope based on God's Word and character that in every trial and difficulty help will come from God. God has promised that when we ask, we shall receive; when we knock, the door shall be opened; when we seek, we shall find. Learn to share this message with those who are hurting, and remind them that God is swift to help those who are burdened, either to deliver them from their troubles or provide the grace that will enable them to transform their pain into a pearl.

Lord, help me to come alongside a wounded individual and whisper that Jesus cares. Amen.

CARING IS UNDERSTANDING

Ephesians 4:1–16

'... *be patient, bearing with one another in love.*' (v.2)

Caring is helping a person feel understood. Everyone likes to feel understood, but how do we get across to someone who is hurting that we do understand? We do it by giving the person a short summary of the problem as we see it. I stress the word 'short' because there is nothing more inane and pointless than to repeat people's statements back to them verbatim. A short summary shows the person that you have grasped and comprehended their problem, and gives them the reassurance that, even though you might not have a solution, at least you understand. And being understood is as helpful to the emotions as good advice is to the mind.

Father, help me to be skilful at this task of helping people feel understood and cared for. Amen.

COMMON CHRISTIAN PROBLEMS

Luke 24:13–35

*'As they talked and discussed these things ...
Jesus himself came up and walked along
with them ...' (v.15)*

One of the most common problems Christians struggle
with is doubt. They doubt such things as whether
God loves them, whether He answers prayer and whether
the Bible is true. How do we care for those in doubt? We
must not allow ourselves to be upset or judge them. Keep
in mind, as you listen, that most people's doubts are not
in the mind but in the heart. Some doubts are intellectual
but most are emotional. By that I mean the person may be
carrying a deep hurt which causes them to question the
truth and reality of their intellectual beliefs. Jesus waited,
listened and showed He cared before sharing Himself.

**Lord, teach me to get alongside people and not just
confront them. I must love people before I start giving
them answers. Amen.**

DISCOVERING LIFE'S GREATEST PURPOSE

WHY SUFFERING?

1 Corinthians 12:12–26

----

*'If one part suffers, every part suffers
with it ...' (v.26)*

For centuries Christians have struggled with the
problem of suffering – and there are no easy answers.
How do we care for Christians who are struggling? We
do it by showing that we are willing to take a little of their
suffering and pain into ourselves. By that I mean that we
encourage them to talk out their fears, their anxieties, their
anger, even allowing it to fall upon ourselves. It's not easy
to sit alongside someone who is suffering and allow them to
unload their fears or resentment into your heart. But this,
I believe, is what Paul meant when he said, 'Carry each
other's burdens, and in this way you will fulfil the law of
Christ' (Gal. 6:2).

**Father, Jesus bore my pain and suffering on the cross.
Help me to bear the pain and suffering of others.
For Jesus' sake. Amen.**

MEETING DISCOURAGEMENT

2 Corinthians 10:1–5

'... we take captive every thought to make it obedient to Christ.' (v.5)

Christians often grapple with discouragement. Sometimes this is due to a physical problem such as poor sleeping habits, illness or improper diet. Here a medical examination could be appropriate. Emotions are affected by our thinking. It is impossible, by an act of will, to stop feeling discouraged, but if we work to change our thinking, then the feelings of discouragement often dissolve. So ask what a person is thinking and gently challenge non-biblical thinking. Discouraged people need, more than anything else, to get a new perspective on life, and this can often come from a caring friend who lovingly dares to challenge and help change the discouraged person's thinking and conclusions.

Father, may I be able to come into the lives of others with a kindly word and deep insight so that they may hope in You. Amen.

THE TYRANNY OF THE URGENT

John 11:1–44

----

*'Yet when he heard that Lazarus was sick,
he stayed where he was two more days.' (v.6)*

Some Christians have a problem with pressure and stress. Pressure and stress often arise from what someone has called 'the tyranny of the urgent'. This is a term used to describe the common habit of always doing what is most pressing instead of taking the time to work out a proper order of priorities. If you see that a fellow believer is under pressure, sit down with them and help them re-evaluate their priorities. Jesus was able to recognise the difference between the urgent and the important. What was the urgent need? Obviously to prevent the death of Lazarus. However, what was the important issue? To raise Lazarus from the dead.

**Lord Jesus, teach me how to build proper priorities
so that I, in turn, might teach this principle to others.
Amen.**

OVERCOMING LOSS

Hebrews 12:1–15

- -

'Look after each other so that not one of you will fail to find God's best blessings.' (v.15, TLB)

Loss comes in many ways – a child leaving home, break-up of a romance, death of a loved one, redundancy, a separation or divorce. Each of these situations can bring a sense of grief. Each stirs up feelings of emptiness, loneliness and a sense of bewilderment. It is important that people admit and share their feelings and understand that it is not a weakness to lean on others at such a time. Taking rest and food may not sound like deep 'spiritual' advice but, believe me, it is. Someone should be available for the person to talk with, pray with and share thoughts from the Scriptures.

Father, deepen my compassion and concern for people more and more as the days go by. Amen.

STOP WORRYING

Philippians 4:1–9

- -

'Do not be anxious about anything, but in everything, by prayer and petition, with thanksgiving, present your requests to God.' (v.6)

Feelings of anxiety do not appear to spring from any reasonable cause. We can be anxious without knowing what exactly we are anxious about. Worry, on the other hand, has a traceable cause. When we worry we usually know exactly what we are worrying about. Scripture tells us not to worry. That advice, coming from someone else, might not go down very well, but coming from God, it has point and purpose. God's method is to replace the worry with prayer: 'Instead, pray about everything.' This means that we should spell out the problem to God in as much detail as possible – we replace worry by telling God about it, and then trust Him to take care of the problem.

Lord, this sounds simplistic, but help me to have an increasing confidence in the power of Your Word and prayer. Amen.

A MODEL OF CARE

1 Kings 19:1–21

'Then he lay down under the tree and fell asleep. All at once an angel touched him ...' (v.5)

Notice how God cared for Elijah. First, Elijah's physical needs: Elijah was given food, drink and a chance to rest. Second, he was given an opportunity to get things off his chest. Talking is therapeutic – the more Elijah talked, the more he released his pent-up emotions. The Lord redirected Elijah's thinking, showing him that he was not alone, nor in danger of death. Elijah's problem was twofold: he was overstretched (hence the food, drink and rest) and he was the victim of wrong thinking. The Lord taught Elijah how to think differently – a basic principle in effective caring – and, before long, Elijah was back in contact with people, free from his doubt and depression.

Father, may I learn to care for others in such practical and effective ways that they may be restored in body, soul and spirit. Amen.

SELF-LOVE

Matthew 22:34–40

'Love your neighbour as yourself.' (v.39)

We must learn how to care for ourselves. There are those who think that Christianity teaches that they must love others but not themselves. This is a mistake. Christianity teaches self-love: 'Love your neighbour as yourself.' Notice, I use the word 'self-love' and not 'love of self'. The two are quite different. Love of self is egocentric interest; self-love is healthy personal concern. If you do not love yourself, you would not develop yourself. Those who love others and not themselves, allowing others to sap the life out of them, end up in disaster. On the other hand, as we have seen, if one organises life around the self and becomes self-centred, then that too ends in disaster.

Father, help me understand that self-love and the care of self is valid and important if I am to effectively care for others. Amen.

CARING FOR YOURSELF

Mark 12:28–34

'... Love your neighbour as yourself.' (v.31)

The words, 'Love your neighbour as yourself,' show that we are to be balanced in our caring – you are to care for others as you care for yourself, and you are to care for yourself as you care for others. This saves the caring from being one-sided: caring for others and neglecting yourself, or caring for yourself and neglecting others. I know many Christians who focus on caring for others but who do not have a healthy and balanced concern for themselves. And what happens? In most cases they end up needing the help and attention of others because they are overspent. Look at the life of Jesus. He took time to rest, pray, eat and be with friends.

Father, help me to be a well-adjusted person, so that all my virtues are balanced, and I do not become lop-sided. Amen.

A HEALTHY SELF-CONCEPT

Matthew 10:16–31

'... you are worth more than many sparrows.' (v.31)

The first step to caring for ourselves is to build a proper self-image or self-concept. This is the image we carry of ourselves deep down in our heart. You tell me the way you see yourself and I can almost predict the course of your life, because you will act and behave in harmony with that self-image. If you see yourself as worthless, inferior or inadequate, then this is the way you will act in your relationships. If, however, you see yourself as a person of inestimable worth bought with the blood of Christ, then you will have a deep conviction that you are of value to Him and to His universe.

O Father, cleanse my self-concept this day so that I see myself as a person of worth and value to You. Amen.

THE GLORY OF GOD

1 Corinthians 6:1–20

'Do you not know that your body is a temple of the Holy Spirit ...?' (v.19)

Many Christians regard the body as a hindrance. It is not. God has given us our bodies for a purpose, and we need to treat them with the greatest respect. If you eat to excess then you will end up with excess weight, which will overburden your heart. Exercise is important, too. You must not forget rest or relaxation either, for if you don't rest and relax properly then the instrument of your spirit (the body) will be less than effective. Whether you eat or drink, said the apostle Paul, do all for the glory of God (1 Cor. 10:31) – and the glory of God dwells in a physically fit person.

Father, help me to be a good tenant of Your temple and keep my body working effectively for You. Amen.

TAKE TIME TO BE ALONE

FOR READING AND MEDITATION

Matthew 6:5–15

'... *when you pray, go into your room,
close the door ...*' (v.6)

If you feel guilty about having time to yourself, then it's a pretty good indication that your self-concept needs attention. Spend time alone. Don't fool yourself into thinking that you don't need to get alone with God at a particular time, in a particular place because you can find God all the time and everywhere. If you are to find God all the time, you must find Him sometime; and if you are to find Him everywhere, you must find Him somewhere. Make sure you have your Bible with you and allow God to speak to you through it. Also, listen to music, read a book or go for a walk. Enjoy your own company!

Father, I see that taking time off need not be selfish but prudent, for such times give me a new perspective on caring. Amen.

STAY IN YOUR CIRCLE

Psalm 16:1–11

'I will bless the Lord who counsels me; he gives me wisdom in the night. He tells me what to do.'
(v.7, TLB)

Many people tend to push themselves, or allow others to push them, beyond the boundaries of their humanity or abilities quoting 'I can do everything …' (Phil. 4:13). Now I am the last one to discourage anyone from reaching out to achieve greater things, but we must interpret Paul's words correctly. *The Living Bible* paraphrase brings out the truth: '… I can do everything God asks me to with the help of Christ who gives me the strength and power.' 'Everything God asks me to' – that is the secret. God has a circle for each one of us in which we can best function for Him. Outside the circle is maximum weariness with minimum effectiveness.

Father, help me to be aware of my limitations, and not allow myself to be driven or pushed beyond them. In Jesus' name. Amen.

DISCOVERING LIFE'S GREATEST PURPOSE

DO IT GENTLY

1 John 3:11–24

*'For God is greater than our hearts,
and he knows everything.' (v.20)*

I n a healthy personality where self-love is understood,
whenever a person makes a mistake, they will evaluate
themselves and their actions in a gentle and loving way.
They will feel a degree of disappointment, but they will not
be desolated by it. Those who are overwhelmed by their
mistakes are being too harsh on themselves. How does God
deal with us when we make a mistake? Gently. You must
love yourself in the same way. But one more thing: do you
congratulate and compliment those you love when they
have done something well? Then do the same for yourself.
You care for others – care for yourself, too.

**Father, help me to be as gentle with myself when I make
a mistake as You are with me. Amen.**

DECEMBER 13
BEING A LOVE RECEIVER

FOR READING AND MEDITATION
1 John 4:7–21

----

*'There is no fear in love. But perfect love
drives out fear ...' (v.18)*

Learn to receive love whenever it is offered to you from
others. I say 'learn' because many are able to give love,
but they are unable to receive it. All of us, deep down, long
to be loved, but to experience such love, or to express it in
return, can be threatening. When people get to know us
intimately they get to know our weaknesses, and there is
always the possibility that they will reject us because of
them. So to protect ourselves from possible rejection, we
maintain our distance and subtly push them away. We will
remain stunted and dwarfed in our personalities if we only
give love and do not receive it.

**Father, help me overcome any difficulties I may have
in receiving love by fully opening my heart to others.
Amen.**

DISCOVERING LIFE'S GREATEST PURPOSE

PITFALLS AND DANGERS

Mark 10:17–31

'At this the man's face fell. He went away sad, because he had great wealth.' (v.22)

The first pitfall in caring for others is that of manipulation. We manipulate people when we try to control them and deny them their freedom. When attempting to help someone, you may long to see them act upon your suggestions or implement your advice. You may grieve profoundly when they take an opposite direction, but you must never, never try to control that person, or dominate them to the degree where they lose their freedom. Jesus' love for this young man did not lead Him to violate the man's freedom. He gave him the freedom to accept or reject the message. He loved him enough to respect his freedom.

Father, help me as I develop my role of caring. I don't want to control people – I want to care for them. Amen.

CURB YOUR CURIOSITY

FOR READING AND MEDITATION
Hebrews 3:1–15

'Beware then of your own hearts ... in case you should find that they, too, are evil ...' (v.12, TLB)

Caring involves a high degree of closeness and intimacy. Be careful that you don't become involved in probing a person for information simply to satiate your own curiosity. If you fail to recognise that caring can make you vulnerable to your own sinful tendencies and fantasies, and you do not throw yourself in complete dependency upon the Holy Spirit for assistance, then you might finish up hurting more people than you help. The same Holy Spirit who motivates you to care can protect you from becoming over-curious or voyeuristic. But be ever watchful that your tendencies do not lead you into areas you should not go.

Father, give me clear insight to avoid cloaking my own curiosity with the garments of caring. For Jesus' sake. Amen.

DISCOVERING LIFE'S GREATEST PURPOSE

DISCIPLINED DESIRES

2 Timothy 1:3–14

'For God did not give us a spirit of timidity, but a spirit of power, of love and of self-discipline.' (v.7)

Ateenage friend of mine did a first aid course. After becoming qualified, he spent most of his time eagerly searching for people whom he could help. He persuaded people who didn't have genuine problems that they needed his expert care and attention. I saw several of my friends walking around with bandaged limbs when there was really nothing wrong with them at all! A scratch required a tourniquet, a simple wrist sprain was supported by an arm sling! Make sure the people you try to help really need it, and are not just objects on whom you can try out your new ideas and skills. Discipline is as necessary to effective Christian living as wings are to a bird!

Father, help me to discipline my desires to care so that they work in the most productive and beneficial ways. Amen.

CARE – ONE AT A TIME!

Proverbs 2:1–10

'He shows how ... to find the right decision every time.' (v.9, TLB)

Begin by caring for one person – and one only. No one has been given a responsibility to care for the whole world. Our task is to care for the person near us who is in need. Jesus helped people one at a time. There were occasions certainly when He preached to the multitudes and fed the thousands, but in the Gospels, there are no fewer than nineteen private conferences that Jesus had with people, thus illustrating the importance of helping people one at a time. Later on the circle of your caring can be widened. You will not be able to care for everyone, but you will be able to care for someone.

Father, thank You for reminding me that the way to care for people is to care for them one at a time. Amen.

CARING FOR THE FAMILY

1 Timothy 5:1–8

'But anyone who doesn't provide for his own relatives ... especially those living in his own family, has no right to say he is a Christian.' (v.8, TLB)

Nothing is so pathetic,' said one writer, 'than a dedicated Christian who has become so concerned in caring for other people that he or she has forgotten the family and lost the respect of people at home.' It is so easy to get involved in 'Christian ministry' and miss out on one of life's most important ministries – caring for one's family. I have come to see that the home has almost as high a priority as the Church in God's scale of values. If God permitted me to have my life over again, I would concentrate on giving equal if not more time to my family than I would give to the Church.

Father, may I care for those inside my home as much or more than I care for those outside my home. Amen.

LEARN TO LET GO

Acts 8:26–40

'The Holy Spirit said to Philip, "Go over and walk along beside the chariot!"' (v.29, TLB)

When I had my first bicycle I quickly got on it, pedalled forward and promptly fell off! My father came alongside and supported me until I could manage on my own. This is what happens in caring. We come alongside a person for a while, hold on and walk with them, so to speak, until we know that they can make it alone. Then eventually we slowly let go, and the person goes on without our help. How did the Ethiopian view Philip's withdrawal? Philip had done his work well – the Ethiopian 'went on his way rejoicing'. We must learn to withdraw when people can manage without our care.

Father, teach me not only how to come alongside people and support them, but also when to let go. Amen.

DISCOVERING LIFE'S GREATEST PURPOSE

BODY CARE

Acts 12:1–17

'... *the church was earnestly praying to God for him.*' *(v.5)*

There is no such thing as do-it-yourself Christianity. The message of the New Testament is that Christians should link themselves with other Christians so that they can give one another prayer and spiritual support. Don't try to care for others without making sure that you have some strong spiritual back-up in the prayers of the Church or at least a group in the Church. From time to time, you need people not only to pray *for* you but to pray *with* you. There will be times of failure, discouragement and difficulty when the prayers of a closely-knit group or fellowship can make all the difference.

Father, place me alongside those whom I can support and who can support me in this vital ministry of caring. Amen.

A SOCIETY OF THE CARING

FOR READING AND MEDITATION
Hebrews 10:19–39

'... let us consider how to stir up one another to love and good works ...' (v.24, RSV)

Our primary responsibility as Christian carers is to help other believers come to maturity (Gal. 6:10) so that we present to the world a model of what care and concern can accomplish in human society. It goes without saying that Christian care should not be limited to fellow believers: it begins there but then flows out to the world. The Church is one society that is structured and designed by God for caring. It is the destiny of the Church to show the world what real caring is all about. We have come to the kingdom for such a time as this (Esth. 4:14).

Father, help every one of us – Your redeemed children – to become examples of unlimited caring. For Jesus' sake. Amen.

'I WILL BUILD MY CHURCH'

FOR READING AND MEDITATION
Matthew 16:13–19

'... I will build my church ...' (v.18)

The Church holds a unique position in the world as it functions against the background of a caring God who overcomes evil with good, hate with love and rebellion with a cross. Because God cares, we must care too. Unfortunately, however, the contemporary Christian Church is far from being the kind of Church God wants it to be. The Church may have its problems and difficulties, but it will ultimately prevail because Jesus said He would build it. So let's take heart, for no matter how difficult things are in your local Christian community, God is committed to bringing His true believers through to victory. And this is not just triumphalism: this is reality.

Father, may I work for You in Your Church knowing that I am involved in an enterprise that cannot fail. Amen.

WHAT IS A CARING CHURCH?

Colossians 1:21–29

'Him we proclaim, warning ... and teaching every man ... that we may present every man mature in Christ.' (v.28, RSV)

A caring church is excited about the matter of bringing its members to maturity. Problems amongst Christians are God's way of highlighting the need for maturity. They help us search out root causes and apply lasting solutions to people's problems, thus making them, and ourselves, more Christlike and more mature in the process. It is quite natural for us to want to run away from a church where there are problems, but sometimes we can be part of the solution. When we assume a personal responsibility for the reputation of Christ and the maturity of our fellow believers in a local fellowship, we advance the cause of Christ in a way that is impossible to explain.

Gracious Father, I have a commission from You to help bring others to maturity and this makes life purposeful and meaningful. Amen.

'MODEL' LEADERSHIP

1 Peter 5:1–11

'... be shepherds of the flock of God ... not as domineering over those in your charge, but providing yourselves models for the flock to imitate.' (vv.2–3, Williams)

A caring church is a church whose leaders demonstrate care and concern for each other, thus setting a good example to the flock. The word 'model' is an interesting one, meaning 'standard', 'example' or 'pattern'. The Church needs shepherds who demonstrate, at a leadership level, their concern for one another, and who 'model' the ministry of caring. Care is demonstrated by concern for each other, by spending time together, not merely in the business meetings of the church, but in relationship-building sessions. Some church leaders I know meet twice a week to build their relationships one with the other because 'the quality of our relationships determine the quality of the whole fellowship'.

Father, enable leaders in Your Church to be good models and examples of Your everlasting love and care. Amen.

A LOVE COVENANT

Matthew 20:20–28

'... whoever wants to become great among you must be your servant ...' (v.26)

A caring church is a church whose members are willing to lay down their lives for others. In my travels I have come across only one church where a commitment was made by every member to place the interests of the other members before their own. I found it in the town of Pusan, Korea. Whenever someone joins this church, either through conversion or moving into the community from elsewhere, all the other members gather round that person. They recite together a covenant that promises to care and serve that person in love. The atmosphere in that church was the most wonderful I have ever experienced in many years of ministry.

Father, help me be the kind of person I want others to be and help me to take the initiative in love and service. Amen.

DISCOVERING LIFE'S GREATEST PURPOSE

INVENTIVE LOVE

1 Corinthians 13:1–13

'Love never fails.' (v.8)

A caring church has an organised programme of love and support. In a truly caring society nothing is left to chance. Problems are anticipated, thought through, and solutions developed. In one church a person has been appointed to oversee care. The one in need would be placed under the care of a support group, ie two or three carefully chosen individuals who will pray, nurse and support the wounded or hurt member until he or she is on their feet again. There is also a caring group trained in the giving of practical help. This group has access to a special fund created by the church to help those in urgent need. Love is inventive, organised and practical.

Father, help our care and love to be organised, inventive and practical. Teach us how to care – to really care. For Jesus' sake. Amen.

SHARING AT A DEEP LEVEL

Romans 15:1–13

'Accept one another, then, just as Christ accepted you ...' (v.7)

A caring church is a church where people are encouraged to share their deepest feelings and hurts without fear of being rejected. Some churches find it difficult to accept people as they are, but only as they want them to be. How sad! The Church is full of people who are not perfect and experience problems that they are reluctant to share because they are afraid of rejection. Instead, they say to themselves whenever they have a problem, 'I shouldn't feel like this' – so they pretend they are all right when they are not. If we care for people, we will give them the freedom to tell us how they feel without the fear of being rejected. God took the greatest love initiative in sending His Son – which we celebrate this season.

Father, help me this Christmas to determine to develop and demonstrate a loving acceptance of people as they are, not as I would like them to be. Amen.

CARING IS NOT OPTIONAL

Hebrews 13:8–21

'Don't forget to do good and to share what you have with those in need, for such sacrifices are very pleasing to him.' (v.16, TLB)

When we love God, and are committed to His cause, then we are not left with the option of deciding whether or not we will care for others. The days of offering sacrifices on a stone altar are long passed, for the Son of God has paid the full atoning price for our sins by His eternal sacrifice on the cross. However, listen to today's text as from the Amplified Bible: 'Do not forget or neglect to do kindness and good, to be generous and distribute and contribute to the needy of the church as embodiment and proof of fellowship, for such sacrifices are pleasing to God' (v.16). Caring is not optional.

Father, I offer You myself to care for others as You have cared and sacrificed Yourself for me. For Jesus' sake. Amen.

AN EPILOGUE

Hebrews 12:14–29

'Look after each other so that not one of you will fail to find God's best blessings ...' (v.15, TLB)

Some years ago a sociologist wrote an article describing what he called the 'helper-therapy principle'. After examining the lives of hundreds who were actively involved in helping others, he discovered that those who help are the ones who are helped the most. There are several reasons for this. When we care for others, we fulfil one of the purposes for our existence and experience the satisfaction that we are functioning in harmony with the laws of the universe. Also we tend to have a clearer perception when handling our own problems. Another reason is that when we reach out to others and make an impact on their life, we experience feelings of deep significance.

Father, thank You for showing me that those who help others are themselves helped. When I give, I receive. Amen.

DISCOVERING LIFE'S GREATEST PURPOSE

DOORS OPEN OUTWARD

FOR READING AND MEDITATION
Revelation 3:7–13

… I have placed before you an open door …' (v.8)

Can loving God and caring for others be an effective formula for living? I believe it can. Actually John, the apostle, reminds us that obedience, love and caring are the primary marks of a disciple of Jesus Christ (John 13:34–35). A woman, who had been through one of CWR's counsellor training courses, said to me, 'Since I committed my life to helping others, all the doors in my personality have been unlocked.' It cannot be otherwise. The doors of the uncaring person all open inward: the doors of the caring person open outward. When we look inward we limit ourselves, when we look outward we expand ourselves.

Father, thank You for the door of caring that is before me. Help me go through it and expand my horizons in You. Amen.

'HE'S MY BROTHER'

Hebrews 13:1–8

'Keep on loving each other as brothers.' (v.1)

What is life's greatest purpose? To love God and to love others. We love others by caring for them. A girl was seen carrying her little brother home after he had fallen and grazed his knee. The little boy was almost as big as her, and as she seemed to be labouring under the burden of his weight, a neighbour said, 'Put him down, my dear. He's too heavy for you to carry.' The little girl replied, somewhat indignantly, 'He's not heavy: he's my brother.' Caring is carrying, and the one you are carrying is your brother. You carry him to your Father who will heal and restore, so your brother one day will be able to carry others also.

Father, thank You for this ministry of caring. It is a heavy burden but a worthwhile burden to see my brothers and sisters made whole.

DISCOVERING LIFE'S GREATEST PURPOSE

National Distributors

UK: (and countries not listed below)
CWR, Waverley Abbey House, Waverley Lane, Farnham, Surrey GU9 8EP.
Tel: (01252) 784700 Outside UK (44) 1252 784700 Email: mail@cwr.org.uk

AUSTRALIA: KI Entertainment, Unit 21 317-321 Woodpark Road, Smithfield,
New South Wales 2164. Tel: 1 800 850 777 Fax: 02 9604 3699
Email: sales@kientertainment.com.au

CANADA: David C Cook Distribution Canada, PO Box 98, 55 Woodslee Avenue,
Paris, Ontario N3L 3E5. Tel: 1800 263 2664 Email: sandi.swanson@davidccook.ca

GHANA: Challenge Enterprises of Ghana, PO Box 5723, Accra. Tel: (021)
222437/223249 Fax: (021) 226227 Email: ceg@africaonline.com.gh

HONG KONG: Cross Communications Ltd, 1/F, 562A Nathan Road, Kowloon.
Tel: 2780 1188 Fax: 2770 6229 Email: cross@crosshk.com

INDIA: Crystal Communications, 10-3-18/4/1, East Marredpalli, Secunderabad
– 500026, Andhra Pradesh. Tel/Fax: (040) 27737145
Email: crystal_edwj@rediffmail.com

KENYA: Keswick Books and Gifts Ltd, PO Box 10242-00400, Nairobi.
Tel: (254) 20 312639/3870125 Email: keswick@swiftkenya.com

MALAYSIA: Canaanland, No. 25 Jalan PJU 1A/41B, NZX Commercial Centre,
Ara Jaya, 47301 Petaling Jaya, Selangor. Tel: (03) 7885 0540/1/2
Fax: (03) 7885 0545 Email: info@canaanland.com.my

Salvation Book Centre (M) Sdn Bhd, 23 Jalan SS 2/64, 47300 Petaling Jaya,
Selangor. Tel: (03) 78766411/78766797 Fax: (03) 78757066/78756360
Email: info@salvationbookcentre.com

NEW ZEALAND: KI Entertainment, Unit 21 317-321 Woodpark Road,
Smithfield, New South Wales 2164, Australia. Tel: 0 800 850 777
Fax: +612 9604 3699 Email: sales@kientertainment.com.au

NIGERIA: FBFM, Helen Baugh House, 96 St Finbarr's College Road, Akoka,
Lagos. Tel: (01) 7747429/4700218/825775/827264 Email: fbfm_1@yahoo.com

PHILIPPINES: OMF Literature Inc, 776 Boni Avenue, Mandaluyong City.
Tel: (02) 531 2183 Fax: (02) 531 1960 Email: gloadlaon@omflit.com

SINGAPORE: Alby Commercial Enterprises Pte Ltd, 95 Kallang Avenue #04-00,
AIS Industrial Building, 339420. Tel: (65) 629 27238 Fax: (65) 629 27235
Email: marketing@alby.com.sg

SOUTH AFRICA: Struik Christian Books, 80 MacKenzie Street, PO Box 1144,
Cape Town 8000. Tel: (021) 462 4360 Fax: (021) 461 3612
Email: info@struikchristianmedia.co.za

SRI LANKA: Christombu Publications (Pvt) Ltd, Bartleet House,
65 Braybrooke Place, Colombo 2. Tel: (9411) 2421073/2447665
Email: dhanad@bartleet.com

USA: David C Cook Distribution Canada, PO Box 98, 55 Woodslee Avenue,
Paris, Ontario N3L 3E5, Canada. Tel: 1800 263 2664
Email: sandi.swanson@davidccook.ca

Courses and seminars

Publishing and new media

Conference facilities

Transforming lives

CWR's vision is to enable people to experience personal transformation through applying God's Word to their lives and relationships.

Our Bible-based training and resources help people around the world to:
· Grow in their walk with God
· Understand and apply Scripture to their lives
· Resource themselves and their church
· Develop pastoral care and counselling skills
· Train for leadership
· Strengthen relationships, marriage and family life and much more.

Our insightful writers provide daily Bible-reading notes and other resources for all ages, and our experienced course designers and presenters have gained an international reputation for excellence and effectiveness.

CWR's Training and Conference Centre in Surrey, England, provides excellent facilities in an idyllic setting – ideal for both learning and spiritual refreshment.

CWR Applying God's Word
to everyday life and relationships

CWR, Waverley Abbey House,
Waverley Lane, Farnham,
Surrey GU9 8EP, UK

Telephone: +44 (0)1252 784700
Email: info@cwr.org.uk
Website: www.cwr.org.uk

Registered Charity No 294387
Company Registration No 1990308

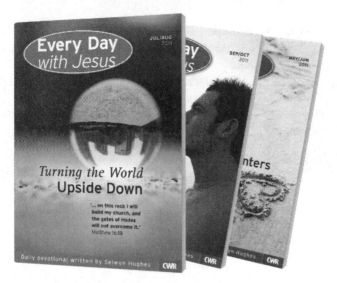

Every Day with Jesus

With around a million readers, this compact bimonthly devotional is one of the most popular daily Bible-reading tools in the world:
• Get practical help with life's challenges
• Gain insight into the deeper truths of Scripture
• Be challenged, comforted and encouraged
• Look at six topics in depth each year
• Get more out of each issue with our free online extras for groups including video and discussion starters.

Also available in large-print format.
£2.75 (plus p&p) each issue
UK annual subscription (6 issues) £14.95 incl p&p
Email subscription £13.80 per year
Prices correct at time of printing.
Visit **www.cwr.org.uk/store**
Also available from your local Christian bookshop

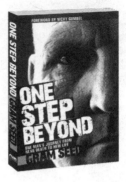

A gripping autobiography that tells of God's amazing love and forgiveness

Take a faith-boosting journey with Gram Seed as he goes from a life of crime and addiction to helping others find new life in God's kingdom.

Gram was written off by family, neighbours, teachers and the police as a lost cause. Your confidence in God's ability to change lives will increase as Gram tells of his miraculous recovery from a six-day coma and how, with the strength of his new-found faith, he now helps other young offenders find God's amazing love and forgiveness.

Both the book and the DVD are effective evangelism tools.

One Step Beyond
by Gram Seed with Andrea Robinson
129x197mm, 180-page paperback
ISBN: 978-1-85345-462-2

One Step Beyond DVD
Powerful drama documentary featuring re-enactments of Gram's life of crime, addiction, hospitalisation, redemption, recovery and ministry. Includes interviews and testimonies.
PSL DVD, 34 mins 6 secs
EAN: 5027957001084